Published by Oxóssi Productions, LLC
2323 De La Vina, Suite 301
Santa Barbara, CA 93105
www.oxossiproductions.com

Project Manager & Creative Director: Amy Hermann
amyhermann.com & sagebrookedesigns.com
Content Editing: Casey DeFranco & Amy Hermann
Copyediting: To Press & Beyond, www.topressandbeyond.com
Cover, Interior, & Logo Design: The Book Designers, bookdesigners.com
Artwork: Refer to Artists' Credits at the end of the book.

The following are trademarked by Oxóssi Productions, LLC: the phrase "Emotional Self-Reliance," the circular logo appearing on the cover and on page 227, and the Oxóssi Productions logo.

Visit oxossiproductions.com for information on an upcoming special edition of this book in full color as well as an eBook version.

The Journey to Emotional Self-Reliance can be ordered through:
www.amazon.com
www.oxossiproductions.com

Library of Congress Control Number: 2017908954

ISBN 978-0-9990582-5-1

The Journey
to
Emotional
Self-Reliance™

*A Guide to Finding
Your Own Way*

GERRY SCHROEDER, PhD

OXÓSSI™
PRODUCTIONS

Contents

INTRODUCTION

- *Are you in a challenging or painful situation?*
- *Are you not sure what to do or how to resolve your dilemma?*
- *Have you turned to your usual sources of information, support, love, and guidance only to discover they are not always available when you need them—or they are no longer working for you?*
- *Do you wonder how you will make the right decisions and support yourself when you are left to find your own way?*

If you answered "yes" to any of these questions, you have come to the right place.

As a psychologist, I have been welcoming people, who are much like you, into my office for the past 40 years. They are up against something difficult or painful, and they do not know exactly what it is or how to resolve it. They feel lost and confused and are looking for direction.

I watch them closely and notice what their facial

expression is telling me. I observe how they walk and move because it reveals how they have tightened their muscles and contained themselves in response to past traumas. Their breathing pattern and energy level lets me know if they are anxious or depressed.

I find myself having great compassion for people's injuries and how they continue to suffer. I grow to love and care about each individual as we work together and listen closely to discover the source of their pain, the desires of their heart, and the choices that are in their best interest.

I have written this book to share with you some of the principles and practices that I have found to be most helpful for people in resolving their personal dilemmas.

This book will *not* give you a direct answer to your dilemma. Rather, it provides a framework that guides you to turn your attention inside yourself for answers and support when your external sources have failed you, and you are feeling alone, lost, and afraid.

It is my hope that this information can help you find your way through your own difficult situations or important decisions.

I have chosen to communicate these teachings to you through a fictional story called "The Journey." I invite you to come along with me on this imaginary journey to work through the dilemma of finding your own way, when you must rely on yourself.

"The Journey" guides you through a series of personal challenges and discoveries. This story might not represent your exact life circumstances or struggles. However, by imagining a different experience than our own—in which something difficult is accomplished—we often gain wisdom and strength that can be helpful in our own lives.

On this imaginary journey, you will be challenged to consider: *"What do I really want from others . . . and how can I give this to myself?"*

As you experience "The Journey" and read the accompanying commentary, you will have an opportunity to gain valuable life lessons and personal practices that will prepare you for learning the Five-Step Practice of Emotional Self-Reliance. When you apply this Five-Step Practice to your own life, you can develop a source of internal guidance that will help you to:

- Take responsibility for your life.

- Support yourself emotionally.

- Make practical decisions that are in your
  best interest.

Only *you* know what is truly in your best interest. You will learn to recognize the clues within yourself to help you identify this truth.

Memorizing the Five Steps is easy—you can read them in less than a minute. However, you will gain little by merely reciting the Five Steps, unless you can also experience them internally and apply them when situations come up that test you. This will take courage, determination, discipline, and practice. Your confidence will grow as you experience success with their application.

Becoming emotionally self-reliant is not something that is mastered immediately. It is an ongoing journey. You may be tempted many times to turn back to your old familiar ways, especially when it is difficult or you feel uncertain. You may find momentary comfort or relief in again doing what you have always done—even though it is not working anymore.

By choosing to continue traveling along on this journey, doing the challenging and rewarding work suggested in the commentary, and learning the Five-Step Practice of Emotional Self-Reliance, you can *establish yourself as your own best guide, advisor, companion, and friend.*

You will then be able to find your own way based on something that exists much deeper inside you.

In life, there are moments of opportunity when a door or window opens briefly and then closes again. You have an opportunity at *this* moment to open yourself to learn something new.

Are you ready? Let's get started.

Your journey begins . . .

The Journey

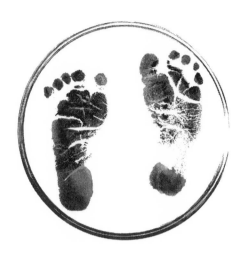

CHAPTER 1

At Home in the Village

Imagine that you are born into a small, harmonious village. There is a great celebration at your birth, as family and friends welcome you. You are given the gift of a healthy body, and you begin to grow. You relax in the comfort and safety of your environment and swallow, with hearty enthusiasm, the nourishing food provided.

You feel so content and secure with the warmth and care of others that you also begin to swallow the things that are said about you. Compliments, such as "beautiful," "charming," "intelligent," and "the bringer of great joy and luck," come to you easily, and you accept these qualities as your true identity.

Your confidence grows as you master the complicated tasks of walking and using language. As you continue to develop, you are said to be "smart," "quick," "caring," "helpful," and "cooperative." You readily take in these descriptions, even though you have little functional experience with what they actually mean.

People express great surprise and laughter at what you say in a spontaneous moment, and you now believe yourself to be "funny" and "entertaining." People appear to like you, and you experience their attention and smiles as "love."

As you move into wider village life, you find that other children enjoy you and want to play with you. You feel welcome and popular wherever you go. One time, you take initiative to accomplish a task on your own without asking permission, and you are recognized as a "leader."

Everything seems to be working out in your charmed life, and you continue to grow into a young adult in this paradise.

The village elders are secretly making plans for you to take a leadership role, and your family hopes you will marry and reproduce yourself in their image of you. You have become the best example of what the village has to offer, and your future appears secure.

Your growing sense of confidence helps you to trust yourself. One day, while relaxing under a shady tree near the village river, an exciting, original idea comes to you. "I want to find my own way. I will leave the village and go seek my fortune."

Chapter 1 Commentary
At Home in the Village

Were you able to begin imagining that you are the main character in this story?

Imagining a Different Life Experience

The childhood that you are asked to imagine is most unusual: you are healthy, welcomed, and supported in such a way that you can prosper. Most of us experience some sort of challenge right from the beginning: we may feel unwelcomed, unloved, or unimportant. We may suffer from illness, poverty, abuse, or family conflict. We may have been born into a family or community where education and opportunity are lacking.

You will discover in our story, as in life, that even in the most ideal circumstances, when everything seems to be going your way, you will encounter conflict. This conflict presents a challenge and an opportunity to learn something new.

Swallowing What Is Given

It is often helpful and necessary to take in and incorporate what is given to us from others. Initially, this is how we survive. As infants, our caretakers feed us and we are nourished. As we grow, we take in language and learn to speak. We absorb ways of relating to one another that help us engage in relationships and feel connected. We are presented information about life and this helps us make sense of it.

Developing Our Early Identity

We are all born into a "village," where our family and community shape our early identity, including our ideas, views of the world, and how we think and feel about ourselves. Others tell us what they like (or do not like) about us. They tell us who we are and who we will become. They tell us how to do things. They tell us what is right and what is wrong. We trustingly swallow and believe what they tell us, because we are initially dependent on them for our survival and do not know any other possibility.

Questions to Consider

• *What were the circumstances that existed at your birth?*

• *How did they impact your early development and identity?*

• *What conditions would you have preferred for your optimal growth?*

Note: "The Journey" and its accompanying commentary may be read in different ways. You may enjoy reading the entire story on its own first, skipping these commentary sections, to drop deeper into the guided visualization and body-centered experience of "The Journey." Then, return later to read the commentary, which is more reflective and psychological. Or, you may enjoy the back-and-forth experience of reading the story along with the commentary for each chapter. Please experiment to discover what approach fits best for you.

CHAPTER 2

Shame

That night at the village gathering, you excitedly tell the people, who have cared for you and given you a sense of your own worth, about your new idea to leave the village and find your own way.

Of course, you have come to expect smiles, support, love, and accolades based on your previous experiences. There is nothing in the universe that could have prepared you for this moment of truth, as a crushing silence falls over the village meeting.

The villagers are dismayed, as they exchange horrified glances! Nobody has ever said this before—this leaving idea—and it comes as a shock to all. They take your idea as a personal affront to them, and they are deeply offended.

The leader closes the meeting early and encourages everyone to go home. No one says a word to you nor looks at you as they leave. You find the silence isolating, as if you have done something terribly wrong. You feel shame. You leave the meeting by yourself, slinking away quietly, wishing you could disappear.

Seeking the shelter of your own home and family for support, you find only more silence. Your mother steps close to you, and you can see the tears in her eyes. You glance over at your grandmother, who scowls at you with cold, threatening disapproval. Your father looks angry.

"What were you thinking to announce such an idea at the village meeting?" your father finally exclaims with disgust. He continues by expressing what everyone in the village has apparently concluded. "How could you be so selfish? What about your family? What about this village that has provided so much for you? Did you consider anyone but yourself?"

You do not have an answer. You suddenly realize that your one original idea is judged by others to be flawed. You are considered "selfish," and it feels like a curse. What to do?

The following days are filled with great distress. Instead of being greeted with familiar smiles and compliments, some people turn and look the other way when you pass, while others come forward to warn you about thinking for yourself. You get the feeling that you are beginning to travel down a dangerous path.

The people who know you and love you express their fears that you might actually try this "unthinkable idea" and perish in your attempt. Others are angry with you, disappointed in you, or repulsed by your presence. You are seen as a threat and some villagers want you to leave, while your closest relatives expect you to stay and care for them, as they grow old. In the end, everyone thinks you have a "bad idea."

It seems each person who knows you has a personal design for how you should live your life. By being yourself and declaring your own ideas, you are suddenly made to feel terribly wrong. What was once a life-sustaining and supportive environment in the village has now become toxic.

You feel alone and stunned by the reaction of others, and yet you are not able to let go of your one original idea.

Chapter 2 Commentary
Shame

Made Wrong for Individual Ideas

When an idea fits for us, we feel energized and full of excitement. We often make the assumption that people who care about us are going to be supportive. However, even in the most ideal situation, there will come a time when these people will disagree with, negate, or shame us for our ideas.

Forms of Shaming

When someone responds to us by turning away in silence, it is a form of shaming that can be extremely punitive and isolating. This is especially true in social situations, when we are seeking approval or trying to be part of a group. Challenging questions or comments can also be shaming. We might hear responses such as, "You don't want that," "That will never work," or "How could you be so selfish?"

Personal Designs

Typically, people we come in contact with have some kind of plan or "personal design" for us. They may think they know what is best for us, or they may want us to be a certain way to make their life easier. These designs or expectations are rarely spelled out in a clear way. They are the agreed-upon beliefs or rules within a family or culture that exist before we are even born. They shape us without our awareness. We typically only realize their existence when we are suddenly made to feel wrong for saying something or doing something that is contrary to these accepted beliefs and rules.

Moment of Truth

It is shocking to experience a sudden change from feeling loved and accepted to being corrected or rejected. A "moment of truth" occurs when we realize that a seemingly wonderful environment of love and support only exists when we go along with these unspoken rules and expectations.

Questions to Consider

- *What are the unspoken rules, beliefs, or expectations that exist in your family or community of origin that you were surprised to discover?*

- *Can you recall a time when you were shamed for expressing an idea or desire?*

- *If so, how did this experience impact your feelings, thoughts, and actions?*

CHAPTER 3

Lost and Confused

What do you do when your village turns against you?

You have not slept well since your announcement at the village meeting. You awaken before the first light of dawn, with a gnawing feeling in your gut and a sense of dread for the day ahead. The restless night is over, and you do not know where to go, what to do, or who to talk to about your loss of comfort and security. Your discomfort is so acute that it drives you out of bed with an impulse to get away.

You decide it is best to leave your parents' house quietly and unnoticed while the household is sleeping. The early morning darkness appears more intense because you feel lost and have no direction. You focus your attention on avoiding obstacles that could crash down and alert others of your attempted escape. You breathe in short, quiet breaths as you feel your way through the darkness using your senses. You exhale cautiously through a small space between your lips.

Without the distraction of sight and interaction with others, your attention turns inward and your body sensations are heightened. Your mouth feels dry with fear and there is an empty, hollow sense in your stomach. As you move with caution, the sounds of your own heartbeat and breath seem louder.

You slip out the door and move away from the house, making your way along a familiar path that leads you toward the outskirts of the village. As you continue to walk, you notice a shift occurring in your body. Your movement away energizes your legs and your strides become faster and longer. As you take in full breaths and your heart rate increases, the tightness inside your chest begins to ease. You realize there is some relief and renewed energy with each step you take to distance yourself from the source of your discomfort.

Breathing in through your nose, you notice the moist, cool freshness of the early morning air. Exhaling fully through your mouth, your jaw relaxes. As your breathing becomes more rhythmic, your stomach softens and you feel warmth spreading down into your hands.

You walk with purpose. As you reach the outer edge of the village, the first light in the eastern sky shines a path out of your darkness.

With the relief of your escape and your initial energy spent, you relax your attention and your walking slows.

You pause and look back toward the village. Immediately, nagging thoughts return to your consciousness. "What about my idea of leaving?" "What should I do?" "How do I resolve this dilemma?" "Who can help me?" "Is there something wrong with me?"

As the unanswered questions flood your mind, the feelings of uncertainty and confusion return. Your body responds as if you are in danger. Your stomach tightens again, your mouth is dry, and your palms are sweaty. This anxiety about what to do makes you feel lost and weak. You remember the feeling that you did something wrong by speaking up and this shame adds to your loss of energy.

In this weakened state, you begin to imagine catastrophes. "What if everyone continues to turn against me?" "What if I venture out on my own and become ill?" "What if I die from a horrible disease because no one is there to take care of me?" These thoughts increase your fear and sense of impending doom. A cold sweat passes over your body as your head continues spinning with thoughts of your demise and eventual death. As this panic overtakes you, it is impossible to think clearly.

Your usual ability to think well of yourself and use your skills at problem solving is momentarily lost and you feel desperate. It seems impossible to remember any past success, and there is a gnawing feeling inside that you are not loved. You feel horribly sick in your stomach, chest, and head, as if you have the flu. Even though you do not know specifically what to do, you feel compelled to move farther away from the location of the original conflict to avoid becoming paralyzed with fear.

You turn away from the village and resume walking. As you do, you begin to feel your stomach relax and you notice that moving farther away from the village brings a sense of relief. You increase your speed and the length of your stride.

You begin to feel excitement and energy in your upper chest and legs, and this inspires you to keep going. It feels as if your chest and legs provide a sense of direction instead of your head.

Chapter 3 Commentary
Lost and Confused

When Others Turn Against Us

When the environment has become toxic and we lack clarity of direction, our discomfort may drive us to get away. This impulse to get away is healthy when we are made wrong and we do not feel welcomed. Other typical responses to this dilemma may include:

- Agreeing with the opinions of others.
- Disagreeing and fighting.
- Explaining our point of view.
- Taking action to demonstrate our position.
- Obsessively overthinking our situation.
- Collapsing and going numb.

Dangers of Overthinking

In moments of shame and self-doubt when we hesitate to act, our mind often becomes flooded with confusing thoughts about our original dilemma. The more we think, the more confused and uncertain we become. Our body then responds to this uncertainty as if we are in danger, which results in fear. This fear then generates worrisome thoughts that can lead to catastrophic thinking, which further amplifies our fear. If we do not take some action, this spiral of increasing fear can result in a panic, where we lose the ability to think clearly and solve problems. Overthinking a problem can take us further away from a solution.

Movement Away from Conflict Decreases Fear

Moving away from conflict is a tactical retreat to reduce fear and regain our composure. It brings temporary relief, although it does not solve the conflict. Distance often helps us see the conflict more clearly and may allow time to discover a solution. The simplest retreat is to take a walk away from the site of the conflict—even if the only immediate option is to excuse oneself to go to the restroom.

Understandably, moving far enough away to fully regain our composure may not be possible in every situation. However, sometimes a momentary retreat can help us recover enough to endure the situation until we have the opportunity to get more distance.

Practice: Retreating from Conflict to Regain Composure

The next time you find yourself in a conflict or toxic environment that is causing you anxiety or confusion, try this tactical retreat, if possible:

1. *Pick a destination and walk with purpose* to get distance from the conflict and focus on something other than your thoughts or experiences of the conflict.

2. *Walk briskly* to increase your breathing and heart rate in order to energize your system and reduce anxiety.

3. *When you begin to experience some relief,* you know you are on the right path to regaining your composure.

Using the Body as a Guide

Our story demonstrates a back-and-forth experience between clarity of direction felt in the body, and confusion from overthinking. Of course, there are situations where it is essential to think through options, consider advice, and use reason to choose the best course of action.

However, when we are confused, additional thinking in that moment seldom solves the problem. By listening to the clues of our body sensations and energy, we can access a source of wisdom that is unattainable through thinking. Throughout our story, you will be encouraged to use your body sensations as your "internal guide" in decision making.

CHAPTER 4

Listening as a Key to Being Present

Pleasure comes to you with your stride, as you continue to move farther away from the village. Soon you are aware of the sound of the rhythmic crunch of your feet on the path. As you listen to each footstep, the confusing thoughts about your future begin to disappear. You find yourself moving forward with open, relaxed breaths of fresh air, as you feel the present moment. You notice the strength of your legs, the ease of your breathing, and the relaxation of your stomach.

After some time, you find yourself walking beside a

river. Now the sounds of your footsteps join in concert with the sounds of the rushing water. The air is cool and refreshing. Trees provide shelter from the midday sun.

As you pause by a calm pool in the river, you catch a glimpse of your own reflection. Your head is tilted forward and down, your shoulders are bowed inward, and your upper back is rounded into a slumping posture. This image is so unfamiliar and surprising that you jolt upward and stand taller. When you do, you feel a breath come up into your chest, and your shoulders relax so your arms hang down lower by your sides. As you bring your head up and draw your shoulders back, you feel bigger. There is now room in your chest to take a deeper breath, and you begin to feel more capable.

Standing taller, you continue walking upward into the mountains toward the origin of the river. After going a fair distance, you feel your legs begin to burn with fatigue, so you sit down by the river.

As you sit quietly, the sound of the water seems to become louder. You listen more intently as the water sloshes around the rocks at your feet, and you can hear a waterfall in the distance. You exhale and adjust your position to become more comfortable. You feel relaxed and at home.

As you stand up to continue following the river, you spontaneously pick up a rock and throw it into the water. You listen to the splash. The pleasure of the experience entices you to repeat it. You pick up another rock and toss it in and hear the sound of a different splash.

Without thinking about it, you start selecting rocks that feel comfortable in weight and roundness. Then you pick a flat rock, toss it sideways, and watch it skip across the top of the water. For a different experience, you pick up a huge rock and heave it into the river with both hands to enjoy the "ker-plosh!"

Each rock has a different look and feel, even though it is part of the same riverbed that channels the water toward its final destination. As you continue to pick up rocks without effort and toss them into the river, you lose track of time and are completely absorbed in the moment.

You notice how quiet your thoughts get when you really stop and listen to the water, the wind in the trees, and the sounds of birds. You are in the present. As you close your eyes to listen with more focused intent, the sounds along the river seem louder, and your thoughts become even quieter.

You feel as though you have entered an altered state of consciousness through this process, and you have a growing sense that you are connected to something bigger than yourself.

You lie down to rest and drift into a sleepy trance.

Chapter 4 Commentary
Listening as a Key to Being Present

Listen to Find Direction in the Present Moment

To be present is to be aware of what is happening right here and now in our body and our surroundings. As our attention becomes focused on present sounds and sensations, we can experience relief from the anxiety and the uncertainty of overthinking. When we are in the present moment, we can make conscious decisions based on listening to our body and our present experience instead of making automatic decisions based on our history or imagined future. Being present also allows us to engage in spontaneous activities or expressive play in which we may discover something new.

Practice: Becoming Present

1. *Slow down and quiet yourself.*

2. *Listen to the sounds around you*—a bird singing, a clock ticking, the hum of the refrigerator, your footsteps as you walk.

3. *Notice your body sensations*—feel the contact between your body and chair or feet and ground; notice whether your muscles feel tight or relaxed; feel your breath coming in and going out.

4. *Bring your awareness back to present sounds and sensations* whenever wandering thoughts begin to dominate your experience.

Practice: Changing Your Posture to Change How You Feel

As you become more present and aware of your body and sensations, you will also become more aware of your posture and its impact on how you feel. You can discover, as in our story, how intentionally changing your posture can change your energy level and feelings. Try the following exercise to experience this relationship between posture and feelings:

1. *Tilt your head* forward and down, roll your shoulders forward, and round your upper back so that you are hunched over.

2. *Notice your breathing* and what body sensations or feelings you have generated.

3. *Now, bring your head up,* sit or stand as tall as you possibly can, draw your shoulders back so that your chest is open, take an easy breath in and then exhale.

4. *What changes do you notice* in your energy level or feelings based on this new posture?

CHAPTER 5

Expressing Anger

You are startled out of your deep and peaceful sleep by the scuffling of black crows directly above your head. Their sudden, loud cries of KAW, KAW, KAW! provoke a fiery irritation that comes up into your chest and upper arms. You jump to your feet with a start and notice a raw, burning tension in your stomach.

Your anger at your interrupted sleep ignites your thoughts as you remember the situation back at the village, where the people you love turned against you in a threatening and dismissive manner. That dreadful feeling of shame has returned.

Without thinking, you grab the nearest large rock and heave it into the river. The thundering splash is so satisfying that you quickly throw a series of rocks into the water, while expressing your anger in a shout. "I hate how you treated me! Get away from me! I did nothing wrong!"

It feels satisfying to express your anger with actions and words. Picking up a rock and throwing it into the river brings relief and even pleasure. As you openly express how you feel, you continue to throw rocks, and the anger that was once burning inside you begins to change.

There is a release from the shame put on you by others. You stand tall and exhale more deeply and then fill yourself again with a good, clean breath of air. You breathe a sigh of relief. Even though the problems in the village still remain, you know there is something you can do to make yourself feel better.

You look around and see a small island in the river, and you imagine throwing a rock and hitting the island. You are irritated when your first attempt misses badly. "I'll get you yet!" you shout. Your anger at the people in your village now has a channel and you become determined to hit the island, even though it appears beyond your reach.

Chapter 5 Commentary
Expressing Anger

Awareness of Anger

In our story, previously unexpressed anger is brought to the surface by a surprise event that causes irritation. When we are made aware of our anger, we can then deal with it. Responding to anger in healthy, productive ways often brings relief and helps us see the world more accurately. Anger is an important emotion that can lead us to clarity, productive action, and a release from shame or depression.

Expressing Anger

This chapter illustrates five healthy and productive ways of processing and expressing anger that can allow us to move forward and make progress, rather than remaining stuck in seething anger, resentment, depression, or shame:

1. *Identify* the general origin of your anger.

2. *Take action* to safely release your anger physically— throw rocks at a target, go for a brisk walk, hit tennis balls, sweep the garage, scrub the floor . . .

3. *Express* out loud what you are angry about while you are safely releasing the anger physically. Keep expressing words and phrases until you have accurately pinpointed the root of your anger. You will know you have hit the target when you have a sense inside yourself, "Yes, that's it!" The intensity of your anger will likely subside once you have expressed your truth. You may then experience a natural exhale of relief and possibly some sadness from your hurt.

4. *Stand tall* and feel the power in your legs as you connect to the truth of your experience that your anger has revealed to you. This will help you feel more capable of standing up for yourself when you are treated in ways that are not good for you.

5. *Channel your anger* into determination to accomplish a personal goal.

Questions to Consider

• *What conclusions did you come to in your childhood about the expression of anger? Are those conclusions useful today?*

• *Which of the five ways listed in the previous section are you more likely to use to process and express your anger?*

• *In what other ways do you respond to your anger? Consider the following common responses to anger:*

Internally Directed Responses to Anger
- Tell yourself you should not be angry.
- Stifle your anger.
- Criticize or blame yourself.
- Withdraw in silence and isolate yourself.
- Become passive.
- Feel sorry for yourself/ Pout.
- Make yourself sick.
- Become sad or depressed.

Externally Directed Responses to Anger
- Make others wrong.
- Do things to make others angry.
- Imagine revenge.
- Physically or verbally attack others.
- Break things.
- Push others away.
- Become sarcastic toward others.
- Develop resentments toward others.

CHAPTER 6
Learning from Experience

Your determination to hit the small island in the river with a rock leads to a conscious decision to pay attention and learn to throw with accuracy.

Your attention now goes to the type of rock you select. You have already learned that a round rock that fits comfortably in your hand is your best choice for a straight throw.

You carefully select a rock and then throw it playfully without thinking—just to see what happens. This throw is easier, more natural, and comes closer to the target. Now you know that relaxing and not overthinking the task are part of the solution. You wonder, "How do I combine these elements with a sense of determination, focus, and control that will result in better accuracy?"

You begin to learn the basic principles of throwing a rock accurately through your many experiences of success and failure.

You find a stance that gives you the best balance and leverage. Planting your feet firmly on the ground, you stand straight and tall, which generates a feeling of competence. You relax by exhaling deeply, beginning from the top of your head to allow your body to soften through your arms, torso, and legs down to your feet. You find it helpful to exhale several times to allow any tension to drain down out of you and into the earth.

You visualize hitting your target. This intention helps you focus on the task at hand. Once you look at your target, you never take your eyes off it until the task is complete.

You discover that a smooth motion of your throwing arm provides the necessary force for covering the distance. The position of your arm and the moment to release the rock are crucial, and you learn these by paying careful attention to the outcome of each throw.

As you become completely focused on this rock-throwing activity, there are no interfering thoughts or reminders of the problems back at the village. You begin to feel comfortable in applying your intention to this present task and you lose track of time. You have entered into a meditative state that brings you an internal sense of peace and increased awareness of the present moment.

There is a thrill through your body when a successful throw hits the target. You let yourself exclaim out loud, "I can do it!" You allow your body to feel how it was done and then celebrate. Today you set a goal of two successful throws out of five attempts before you stop.

You have a growing confidence that you can learn something new from your own determined experience of paying attention and then making corrections.

You look at your reflection in the water, and you can see that you are standing taller. "I can do this. And because I paid attention to how it was done, I can teach others," you say to yourself.

You pause briefly to consider what to do next. You feel hungry and tired. You turn and look toward home, where you know you can easily find food and shelter.

Your initial urgency to get away has subsided. You can breathe easier now, knowing that you can do something to get relief when you are feeling anxious, confused, or angry. You feel better and the shame is gone. Your mind is clear and you are satisfied with the progress of the day. You decide to begin your journey back to the village.

Chapter 6 Commentary
Learning from Experience

Taking Action

Movement away from the site of a conflict can be a helpful action to reduce anxiety or shame and regain composure, as described in Chapter 3. Additionally, we can recover our confidence by becoming successfully engaged in a task where we learn something new from our own experience. Doing something "right" counters the sense that we did something "wrong." We can then come back to the original problem with a fresh perspective and a sense of competence.

Learning from Experience

When we learn something new, we create a memory inside us of the process. We can then use this new experiential knowledge as a model for approaching other important tasks and bigger life goals, such as leaving home or finding a new job. This process of intentionally applying our own experience and knowledge to accomplish a goal increases our confidence and success.

Practice: Learning from Experience

The metaphor of learning to throw a rock from your own experience reveals many helpful elements in approaching a task, refocusing your attention on something other than a current problem, and developing confidence:

1. *Set an attainable goal*—something that you can reasonably achieve in a relatively short amount of time. A larger goal can be broken down into smaller goals.

2. *Focus on your target*—focus on your chosen goal until it is reached.

3. *Adjust your posture*—generate a sense of competence by standing or sitting straight and tall.

4. *Relax*—with long, quiet exhales.

5. *Stay present*—bring all your attention to your present actions.

6. *Make spontaneous attempts that are playful*—try to approach the task without overthinking; have some fun and discover something new.

7. *Pay attention*—to success and failure, pleasure and discomfort.

8. *Make corrections*—apply new knowledge from your experience to each subsequent attempt.

9. *Build confidence*—by celebrating your successes, however small.

10. *Stop on a successful note*—to best internalize your new knowledge.

CHAPTER 7

A Test of Confidence

You walk with confidence back toward the village, head held high and body erect like a tall tree. Your breath comes up into your chest easily, and you relax down to your feet with each exhale.

By listening to the sound of each footstep, you stay present and fall into a smooth, effortless walk. Your legs move easily, and your relaxed arms swing naturally by your sides. There is renewed energy in every step.

You keep your focus on your breath and body movements and remain observant of your surroundings as you walk directly toward the village. The time goes quickly, and you soon find yourself near your home.

Suddenly, you feel your first sense of dread, knowing that nothing has changed in the village and you will not feel welcomed. You bring your awareness back to the newfound confidence inside yourself by remembering your recent successful experiences from your day's journey.

You say a quick hello to the first person you meet. They look away and do not respond. Your energy is immediately diminished, and your posture slumps down. Your breath becomes contracted and shallow. You feel your shoulders rolling forward, as your head drops down until you are looking at the ground. Once again, you feel shame.

Your feelings have abruptly changed from confidence to weakness and emptiness, as if you have done something terribly wrong. You walk quietly now, hoping not to be seen again or confronted as you move back into village life. You realize that maintaining your sense of confidence as you return to the source of your shame is not going to be easy.

As you walk with your head down, you see a rock. Spontaneously you pick it up. You feel how it fits just right in your hand. Without thinking, you look for a target. However, there are others around, and you choose to keep your new rock-throwing skills and sense of accomplishment to yourself.

You believe that people who will not look at you or talk to you will not be interested in what you have discovered. However, there is some comfort in holding the rock and remembering how you can throw with accuracy.

You gather yourself together and stand a bit taller, even though there are still others around who shun you by pretending that you are not there. You remember what you have accomplished, and you begin to feel a growing strength, even though this personal feat is unknown to others. For now, you can begin to act from this experience of confidence without telling anyone about it.

You begin to trust your own skills and counsel as you make a mental note to yourself: *Remember, when others make you feel wrong and try to shame you, come back to something that you know deeper inside yourself.*

That night, before falling asleep, you hold the rock close to you and decide to start your day early and venture even farther away from the village.

Chapter 7 Commentary
A Test of Confidence

Confidence

Confidence is the self-assurance that we can successfully do something. It is an important ingredient for success. Without confidence, we easily find a way to miss the target.

We cannot tell ourselves to have confidence. Confidence is developed through learning new skills, solving real problems, and knowing how we successfully accomplished a task so that we can repeat it. Instructions or guidance from others can be helpful along the way. However, in the end, confidence is only established when we can successfully do something new or difficult without help.

Confidence Is Ever-Changing

It is not easy to maintain a high level of confidence. We can quickly change from being full of confidence to feeling empty and weak from self-doubt when someone corrects us, looks at us with distain, or belittles our accomplishments. Our confidence also rises and falls on a daily basis with our own assessment of our performance. It is especially challenging for us to maintain confidence when returning to the context of a previous trauma where we experienced shame.

Confidence and Posture

Our confidence is often reflected in our posture. We convey confidence when we hold our head high with an upright posture and breathe easily. A lack of confidence is revealed by a slumping posture, contracted shallow breathing, shoulders rolled forward, and head facing down.

Practice: Regaining Confidence

1. *Challenge criticism* by stating, "Now wait a minute, let me think about this."

2. *Review past successes* to generate positive feelings about yourself.

3. *Comfort yourself* by holding or looking at an object that symbolizes a past success.

4. *Adjust your posture* to stand tall with your head held high and softly exhale.

5. *Take action* by returning to a task that you know you can accomplish successfully.

6. *Approach the challenging task* from a place of quiet confidence that with small steps, practice, and paying attention, you can learn something new.

CHAPTER 8

Swallowed Identity

You are awakened in the night by a dream. You have
a dreadful feeling. Your stomach is tight; you are sweating
and feel nauseated. The dream itself is of a peaceful, pleasant
scene in nature: there are baby birds sitting in a nest being
fed by a parent. But there is something about this interaction
that repulses you.

You replay in your mind the image of the young birds
opening their mouths wide to swallow whatever they are fed.
With eyes closed, they take in what is given without tasting
or considering the content.

You suddenly realize what the dream means to you and
why it has given you such a dreadful feeling. As an infant,

you trustingly gulped down food provided by your caretakers, just as these birds did. And, because you learned to swallow what was given, you also readily swallowed compliments, ideas, and identities provided by others, as if they were your mother's milk. They were easy for you to accept as truth without thorough examination, critical thinking, or true knowledge of their meaning.

But how could you possibly trust the wonderful things that were said about you by these people, when the one original idea that you shared with them was greeted with disapproval?

You rise quickly, go outside under the open sky, and begin to puke. The early identities that you trustingly swallowed now make you sick and you feel revolted by them. As you bend over to retch out these undigested identities, there is some relief.

You vomit again and realize that the conclusions you came to about yourself have poisoned you because they were based on what someone said, rather than something that was learned or confirmed by your own experience. You vomit once more to fully empty yourself and the false sense of shame also comes pouring out.

The feeling that you did something wrong by stating your heart's desire is gone. You remind yourself to pay attention to your own experience before you believe what you are told. And then, to make your resolve stronger, you speak out and say, "I will become a picky eater and notice carefully what information is presented about me. I will test it with a small bite to determine if it rings true to my experience before swallowing. If it does not agree with my experience, I will spit it out."

With your newly found realization, you know there is safety from taking on false identities that are not based on your own experiences.

Chapter 8 Commentary
Swallowed Identity

Conflict of Identity

A swallowed identity works for us as long as we continue to go along with the unspoken rules and beliefs of our family and community. However, as we develop and have new experiences that do not match what we were originally told about others and ourselves, we become lost and confused as we experience conflict about what is true. We may at first doubt ourselves: "There must be something wrong with me!" and then we may doubt others: "Did they tell me the truth in the first place?" This confusion is our first clue that something is wrong.

Wisdom from Dreams

When we are lost, confused, and looking for direction, dreams can be a helpful source of information. They offer clues to unresolved questions in our lives. But like many mysteries, they require reflection and interpretation. When we discover the message communicated through our dreams, it can help us come to a new understanding of our present situation.

Wisdom from Body Sensations

Consider the possibility that the body does not lie. We know when we are hungry, tired, interested, bored, amused, afraid, sad, or happy—based on our body sensations. We also know when we have swallowed information about others or ourselves that is *not* true: we may feel sick as we experience physical reactions in our gut, chest, head, or perhaps skin. These physical sensations or "body sig-nals" are undeniable, even if we do not clearly understand what caused them. When we listen and pay attention to these sensations, we have additional information to help us discern what does or does not ring true for us.

Questions to Consider

- *Do you remember a situation when your body signaled that something was wrong, even though you did not know what it was?*

- *If so, where did you sense this in your body and what did it feel like?*

- *What additional information or experiences helped you clear up your initial confusion and discern the truth?*

- *What conclusion had you originally swallowed that was not true for you?*

CHAPTER 9

Identity Based on Experience

While sitting quietly and looking at the starry sky, you remember the rock that you carry with you. It fits in your hand just right, and you feel connected to your own experience of accomplishment. In leaving to find your own way, you have discovered your courage. By channeling your anger into determination, you feel transformed. You have a sense of competence in being able to learn something new, and confidence to hit a chosen target. A new identity is beginning to form based on your own personal experience.

Without awakening anyone, you go back inside to quietly gather some things together, slip out of the house, and make your way through the village. It is dark, but now you can see the way clearly, because your senses are open. You trust yourself and listen to detect things that are unseen.

After you reach the outskirts of the village, you begin to walk quickly and your legs gather energy as you move farther along the trail. You feel your breath rising in your chest and you exhale deeply. Your hips move easily as you lift your knees to extend each step. As each alternating foot comes down to the ground, you roll it forward from heel to toe and push off with power. There is increased energy in your lengthening stride.

Your determination to move away from the village now is similar to when you first set your target and threw the rock. You have a goal to find your own way, even though you do not know the details of how this will be done. You can feel this is the time to trust yourself and base your identity on your own experiences and on the sensations you feel in your body rather than the directions of others.

You are leaving home based on your determination, skill, and confidence to pay attention to your own internal direction and then make adjustments along the way that will bring you closer to your goal. There is a growing sense of relief and joy in your movement away from the village. It just feels right for you.

You walk faster, with head erect and eyes level, to take in everything around you. You feel better with this new sense of self that is based on your own experiences, not on some old identity that you swallowed whole without really digesting or understanding.

You are developing a secret determination to trust your own ideas and keep them to yourself. You are also trusting your own experience, and you now know that you are on the right path when your energy increases and you feel yourself growing bigger and more confident.

You walk farther up the river today and notice a smaller stream entering the river from higher in the mountains. Based on your own interest, you choose to follow that stream to find its source. As the sound and feeling of the water draw you, you carefully follow the stream as it takes you higher. You find yourself walking into a fresh-smelling, tree-lined area, and you move to an open spot under a large tree near the stream.

The shade under the tree invites you and the scent is welcoming. You stop to rest because of the increased fatigue in your legs. You trust yourself to pause and look around to assess the relative safety of this resting spot.

You sit down quietly near the stream, so that you can hear it clearly and feel its pulse of energy coming down from the mountains above. There is something magical about this spot that draws you to remain and wait quietly. You make yourself comfortable. As you exhale deeply down to your feet, your senses open to your surroundings and you listen.

Chapter 9 Commentary
Identity Based on Experience

Swallowed Identity Versus
Identity Based on Experience
Imagine as a child being told, "You are so smart!" You then begin thinking of yourself as a smart person, even though you are not sure what that means. Now imagine instead that you take a difficult math test in the fourth grade. You solve all the problems without a struggle. Afterwards, the scores are posted and you have the top score in the class. You now *know* you are smart at math. In the first example, you develop a swallowed identity of "being smart." The second example brings you to the conclusion that you are smart based on your experience of accomplishment.

The chart on the following page summarizes the differences between a swallowed identity and an identity based on experience.

Questions to Consider

- *What aspects of your early identity developed by swallowing what someone said about you?*

- *What new or different conclusions have you come to about yourself since then, based on your own experiences and accomplishments?*

Swallowed Identity	**Identity Based on Experience**
Directed by Others	**Self-Directed**
1. *Identity originates from an outside source* when others tell you who you are and you believe them.	1. *Identity is generated from an inside source* when you learn who you are from your own experiences.
2. *You look to others* to tell you what you should do. You trust others and follow their directions.	2. *You determine* what to do based on your own interest, assessment, and level of energy in your body.
3. *You trust others* to tell you what is true and you believe them without question.	3. *You trust your own experiences* and body sensations before you believe what you are told.
Consequences	**Consequences**
1. *Learn to depend on others* for identity and direction.	1. *Learn to be self-reliant* for identity and direction.
2. *Identity is fragile* because those who provided it can take it away.	2. *Identity is reliable* because it is rooted in your experience.
3. *Others label your feelings* for you.	3. *Feelings are generated* by the experiences you have in your body.
4. *Others define* your accomplishments and tell you what is important.	4. *You are connected to your own experience* of accomplishment and what is important.
5. *You feel confused and in conflict* when new experiences do not match what you were told.	5. *You have clarity* when you trust your experiences and body sensations to form new conclusions.
6. *You believe* you are on the right path when you please others.	6. *You know* you are on the right path when your energy increases and you feel determination, confidence, and joy.

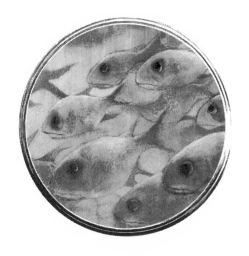

CHAPTER 10

Trapped by Fear and Group Identity

A flash of reflective light directs your attention to small fish swimming in the water. First you see one, and then you see many. They are all about the same size, and they swim in unison with coordinated movements, as if choreographed by some unknown source. None of them strays far from the group. Sometimes you find one that swims away just a little, but quickly rushes back.

You begin to wonder about their experiences as they do exactly the same movements together. It looks to you like "friendship" or "safety in numbers." It appears that the key is to stay in the middle of the school, thinking, *Please eat my siblings on the outer circle so I can live to tell about it.*

Even though you assume it is in their best interest to stay together for survival, you feel bothered that no one leaves the group. As you look closely at the fish, you notice their eyes and the shape of their mouths. Their frozen expressions appear "glum." You feel sad for them, because you imagine their existence is driven by fear and there are no individual adventures for them as they stay with the same friends, rules, and way of living.

You remind yourself that these are just fish, and they are following their instincts. So why do you feel sad?

Then you realize that your sadness is actually about your own life, living in the village, going by village rules, and never venturing forth. You feel a desire to break away from the group and find your own way, even though it might be dangerous. You begin to feel again how you want to trust your own sense of direction to discover something new.

It becomes clear to you why no one ever leaves the village. There are benefits of staying in a group, just as there are for the fish. People are afraid to leave the old familiar ways of village life that provide comfort and security. They do not know their individual way and are not willing to trust themselves to find it.

You understand now that it is the fears of the other villagers that were ignited when you expressed your idea of leaving. They projected their fears onto you and made you feel wrong, rather than admitting they were afraid to go themselves.

You breathe a sigh of relief, knowing there is nothing wrong with you or your idea of leaving. If they want to stay, let them stay. You resolve to leave the group and go your own way. This is your new target.

You test your conclusion by saying it out loud: "I will leave the village." You listen to the sound of this statement. You listen to feel if it rings true inside yourself. And you ask again, "Is this really true? Is this really what I want?"

Then you lean back and close your eyes to listen at a deeper level for your true desire. You drift into a deep sleep to the sound of the stream, knowing that the freedom to go your own way is a choice that you can make for your life.

Chapter 10 Commentary
Trapped by Fear and Group Identity

This is not a chapter about fish. It is about seeing ourselves more clearly when we watch the fish and acknowledge we have become trapped in our own original group identity and are afraid to change. It describes the struggle to leave the familiar existence of our original home and face the uncertainty of finding our own way.

Identifying with the Group

We are born into a family and culture and adapt to our circumstances. We identify with our group as we all go the same direction, in the same way, just as the fish. As we swallow ideas and beliefs that are fed to us, they become part of a familiar way of experiencing our world. With repetition, we then automatically act out our usual ways of dealing with life. Because our original survival was based on this connection to family and culture, it is difficult to do something different or to leave. We feel more secure when there are other people who agree with our thinking and choices. The group provides support and reinforcement to continue doing things the same old way.

Trapped by Fear and Group Identity

We might try to venture forth to find our own way, but when it gets difficult or we become uncertain, we quickly go back to our original group for comfort and safety. We do not know our individual way and are afraid we will not make it on our own. We then resolve to stay with the group and settle back into a sense that "This is just the way it is." We listen to the advice of others and learn to ignore the quiet voice inside that says, "I want to find my own way." We often feel empty, sad, or irritated while remaining trapped in this group identity.

Letting Go of the Familiar

It takes a conscious, concerted effort, along with courage and determination, to let go of our group identity and the old familiar ways that do not serve us anymore. It also requires a system of Emotional Self-Reliance to provide the support and guidance needed for this individual journey.

Testing New Conclusions

When we have an idea to try something new or different, it is helpful to test it first to find out if it really fits for us. We can do this by stating the idea and carefully paying attention to the response from our body.

Practice: Testing an Idea

1. *Say your idea* out loud.

2. *Listen to the sound of your voice.* Is it strong and clear or shaky and doubtful?

3. *Determine if the idea rings true inside* by noticing if you:
   - are curious to explore the idea further.
   - feel excitement in your chest.
   - find yourself smiling.
   - feel inclined to say, "yes!" or "this fits for me!"
   - feel energized to take action.

4. *Check your conclusion* by asking, "Is this really true? Is this really what I want?"

5. *Listen at a deeper level* for your true desire by again noticing your body's responses to your idea.

CHAPTER 11

The Little Red Hen

You awaken to the sounds of the stream bubbling and gurgling its way down the slope of the mountain. The sun warms your forehead as you stretch and relax with a gentle exhale of breath. As your thoughts return to your decision to leave, a memory of a pleasant experience at a past village meeting comes pouring back into your consciousness.

A wise, old woman stood up and wanted to tell a story. She was quite excited as she recited her version of "The Little Red Hen."

ↄ

While scratching in the courtyard looking for food, the little red hen becomes exuberant and cackles loudly, "I found some food! I found some grains of wheat!"

Then the wise, old woman crowed loudly as she scratched the dirt and flapped her arms like wings, and she continued her story.

The little red hen then looked around the village and asked, "Who will help me plant these grains of wheat so they can grow?"

"Not I," said the rooster. "My strut needs a booster."

"Not I," said the duck. "Work seems like yuck."

"Not I," said the hog. "I'm digging in the bog."

"Okay," said the little red hen, "I'll do it myself." And she did.

As the plants grew tall and the harvest was near, the little red hen asked, "Who will help me harvest this wheat?"

"Not I," said the goose. "I'm busy standing tall to be any use."

"Not I," said the rat. "I'm hiding from a cat."

"Not I," said the mouse. "My cousin is visiting at my house."

"Okay," said the little red hen, "I'll do it myself." And she did.

When she had harvested the grains of wheat, the little red hen asked, "Who will help me grind this wheat into flour to bake bread?"

"Not I," said the cow. "I'm busy chewing my cud now."

"Neigh," said the horse. "I'd rather swish my tail and run the course."

"Not I," said the goat. "I'm cleaning my coat."

"Okay," said the little red hen, "I'll do it myself." And she did.

When it was time to bake the bread, the little red hen asked, "Who will help me bake the bread?"

"Not I," said the lizard. "I'm training to be a wizard."

"Not I," said the donkey. "I'm practicing to bray on key."

"Not I," said the sheep. "I'd rather sleep."

"Okay," said the little red hen, "I'll do it myself." And she did.

She baked bread and its delicious smell wafted throughout the village. Now the animals came and offered their help, as they said, "We'll help you eat your bread."

And the little red hen said, "No! I'll eat it myself." And she did.

⤳

When the wise old woman finished her tale, the villagers laughed loudly and clapped their hands as she demonstrated again how the little red hen stood tall, puffed out her chest, and proclaimed, "I'll do it myself!" And then, the wise old woman repeated the conclusion several more times to great applause and cheers.

In the following days, there was sporadic laughter heard around the village as people spontaneously practiced the dance of the little red hen, followed by the proclamation, "I'll do it myself!"

Chapter 11 Commentary
The Little Red Hen

Pleasant Memories

Often at the moment we feel ready to leave a toxic situation, a memory of a pleasant experience related to this same situation returns. We might then recognize that not every aspect of the situation is toxic. These thoughts may cause us to question our decision to leave or to make the changes we are considering. We may find ourselves thinking, "It's not so bad" or "I don't want to lose that good part, so maybe I can find a way to stay and make it work."

Questions to Consider

- *Have you had this experience of pleasant memories pouring into your mind just at the moment you have decided to leave a situation that is not healthy for you?*

- *If so, how did these pleasant memories affect your decisions and progress with your plans?*

Finding Meaning in a Story

People can come to different conclusions based on the same story. A story is always open to interpretation. One part or aspect of the story might resonate with you and another part might not.

Questions to Consider

- *Do you recall hearing or reading a version of "The Little Red Hen" in your childhood?*

- *What was the take-away message most emphasized in your family?*

- *What stands out to you now in reading this version of "The Little Red Hen"?*

CHAPTER 12
I Will Do It Myself

As you stretch and remember other pleasant times in the village, you begin to smile. The warmth of your smile passes through your chest, belly, and legs. You find yourself repeating quietly "I'll do it myself," as you stand up and begin to imitate the wise old woman and her chicken dance.

You stretch your arms as if they are wings, kick your legs backwards as if scratching in the dirt, stand tall with your chest puffed out, shake your feathers, and say, "I'll do it myself!"

You repeat this phrase just as you first heard it and some pride comes up into your chest as you proclaim, "This fits for me!" You declare it more loudly and walk about, connecting with the power of this statement in your body. Just as you developed a sense of determination to hit a target with a rock, there is a growing determination to leave your village and find your own way.

You recall village discussions about the other lessons of "The Little Red Hen," and you know they also apply to your life. You realize that leaving will take more than just the attitude and determination to do it yourself. It will take planning and hard work.

This task will be difficult, just as growing the wheat and making the bread was for the little red hen. However, you know that step-by-step, you can make progress toward this target of leaving, in the same way you learned to throw a rock with accuracy.

You feel inspired to move forward through your own initiative. You do not want to wait for others to help you, support you, or do the hard work for you. You feel encouraged as you recall your recent success of acquiring experience and knowledge on your own.

You remember, "I did it myself" as you puked out the old untried identities that made you sick. There is also a memory inside you of, "I did it myself," as you walked farther and farther away from the village and created a new world of experiences. And you know, "I did it myself," as you found the fish swimming in a school and realized the truth that no one ever left the village because of their fear. You understand that the villagers found relative safety in staying with the group, but there was also a slow death in mindlessly doing the same thing as their neighbors.

You choose to do it yourself and stay alive, no matter how difficult. There is a new sense of peace inside. You have a goal to leave, you know what it feels like to be determined, and you realize that doing it yourself feels right. You pick up the rock again and feel how well it fits in your hand. There is comfort in truly knowing what fits for you from your own experiences.

You clear your throat and know you have something to say out loud with confidence: "I will do it myself. I will leave the village." You stand a little taller and feel the energy in your legs. Now you continue your walk upstream with head held high, eyes level, and arms swinging comfortably.

Your energized walking pace takes you higher into the mountains away from the village. You eventually arrive at the top of a ridge and begin rhythmically walking down the other side. This is an area where you believe no one else in the village has ever gone. There is a taboo against going over the ridge to the other side.

You find a growing confidence inside yourself as your stride lengthens and you look forward to exploring new territory with interest and excitement.

"I will do it myself," comes back to you stronger than ever.

Chapter 12 Commentary
I Will Do It Myself

I Will Do It Myself

The conclusion "I will do it myself" is at the heart of our intention to be self-reliant. It is a determined attitude to move forward and reach our goal through our own initiative rather than waiting for others to support us. Of course, external support can be helpful and at times necessary. However, it might not be readily available. Being willing and ready to do the hard work ourselves is liberating!

Practice: Warming Up for Action with Movement

As demonstrated in our story with the "chicken dance," physical movement is helpful to become energized to take action toward your goal.

1. *Bring a goal into your awareness.*

2. *Get up and engage your arms, legs, and torso* to start walking, dancing, or moving to increase your energy as you picture your goal.

3. *Do not take yourself too seriously here.*

4. *Have some fun* and try saying out loud, "I will do it myself!"

5. *Notice whether you feel more energized* to take action toward your goal.

CHAPTER 13

Fear of the Unknown

Your senses are sharpened because of your confidence and energy. You become keenly aware of everything around you. You take in the surrounding scenery of trees, rocks, bushes, and the occasional tracks of familiar animals. You smell the air and hear the sounds of rustling leaves, the call of birds, and the crunch of your own steps as you walk farther away from the discomfort of village life.

You find yourself smiling as your pace quickens. Your stomach relaxes and you exhale deeply. Your pelvis tilts forward, so your knees lift higher allowing your legs to stretch into longer strides. Your walking is rhythmic and effortless. Your feeling of well-being and your increased energy make you aware that your movement away from the village is right for you. It is easy to continue making your way down the other side of the ridge.

Suddenly, on the path in front of you, you catch sight of something that causes you to freeze in your tracks with terror. Your heart pounds, your mouth goes dry, and you can barely whisper the words, "Human footprint!"

You duck your head and hold your breath as you crouch low to look for any danger that might be lurking around you. You do not see anything, so you carefully examine the footprint, looking for clues as to who might have left this track along your path.

According to your knowledge from village lore, there are no people living on this side of the mountain! The panic inside you is now palpable: your heart pounds harder, your breath is short, your mouth is dry, and your hands feel sweaty as you hold your body rigid with intense fear.

Your first impulse is to run back to the village and tell people what you have seen. But you stop to consider this option. People have already turned against you because of your ideas. It would be easy for them to discredit you. And to make matters worse, you have now disobeyed village rules by venturing into this unknown territory. You could be punished for your disobedience.

You momentarily lose your sense of direction, your brain feels numb, and you cannot think clearly. You try to calm yourself by saying out loud, "I will be okay," but this does not work. Your body signaled imminent danger when you saw the unknown human footprint on this forbidden side of the mountain. You feel overwhelming uncertainty and your body reads uncertainty as danger. With no immediate plan on how to proceed, you feel only mindless panic.

Finally, you remember to stand still and listen. You hear your shortened breath and the pounding of your heart in your chest. You remember to release a longer exhale and that gives you some relief. You exhale more deeply and your shoulders begin to come down and your belly softens. "This feels better," comes out as a soft murmur from your slightly open mouth.

You take the time to look around, and your surroundings become more clearly defined. You see another matching footprint the same size and shape. You feel relief as you conclude that, so far, it appears there is only one person. You notice sand has blown over the edges of the footprints, which tells you they were not made today. Another exhale of relief! A little information has diminished your fear of imminent danger.

You retrace your steps and find the path you took to arrive here and you cautiously make your way back to the top of the ridge to more familiar territory. You are still wary, but your tight, fearful movements have become more relaxed. You have survived, for the moment, but you continue looking into the trees and surrounding hillsides for signs of the unknown stranger.

At the top of the ridge, you feel comfort in returning to the familiar. First, your discomfort had driven you away from the village. Now, your fear of unknown danger is driving you back to the village for support and relative safety in numbers, just like the school of fish. Remembering how a single fish would venture away from the school only to dart back to the group in a panic brings a smile to your face.

Chapter 13 Commentary
Fear of the Unknown

Surprises on Your Path

Often just at the moment when we are experiencing success, feeling full of ourselves, and moving forward with ease, there comes a surprise—something that disrupts our plans, creates uncertainty, and triggers fear.

Fear and Panic

Our body has the same fear response when we encounter real or imagined danger. Escalating fear can lead to panic. The subsequent fight, flight, or freeze response is activated in our bodies as adrenaline is dumped into our system. This response hijacks our common sense and rational thinking as a rapid heartbeat, shortness of breath, and a tight stomach consume us.

Practice: Managing Fear and Panic

The following steps can help calm your system and refocus your brain in an immediate crisis:

1. *Exhale slowly and fully* to override short, anxious breathing.

2. *Look and listen* to gather more information from your immediate surroundings.

3. *Bring your brain into focus* by using critical thinking to assess the situation:
   - Is the danger real or imagined?
   - If real: Is it immediately life-threatening? What is the quickest way to safety? Activate a plan without losing sight of your original goal.
   - If imagined: Exhale again and reassure yourself that you are okay. If needed, return to a familiar and safe environment.

CHAPTER 14

It Is Never Completely Safe

Your fear of the unknown is, for the moment, stronger than your courage to escape the village you have known your whole life. You can now understand why no one has left the familiar safety of the village to find their own way. The unrecognized footprint is your first clue of possible danger, and you watch carefully for any further signs to determine who had walked there.

You ask yourself if the printmaker is a friend or an enemy, and what you would do if you should encounter him or her directly. You cannot help but wonder if this person is watching you.

The unknown charges your imagination with fear, and the fear creates even more dangerous possibilities in your mind. As you review this imagined danger, your body responds again with the same fear signals you first noticed when sighting the footprint. All your senses remain focused for any further clues to the stranger.

Without warning, a new, unexpected danger abruptly stops you in your tracks again, and you jump back. "Rattlesnake!" is uttered from your pursed lips.

The snake is directly in your path and it immediately coils with its head pulled back ready to strike. The buzzing tail clearly warns you to stay away. You fight the panic to yell and run, because you remember where there is one rattle-snake there could easily be others.

You do not move except for your barely perceptible breath, which is short and tight. "Big one!" you whisper, as you calculate his length to be from your feet to your upper chest. You estimate the distance he can strike and then you relax a bit knowing you are just out of range. You also know he will not follow you but only wants to warn you not to step on him. Your quick calculations bring relief that you are relatively safe.

You carefully start walking backward—making sure that in your tenseness you do not fall or step on a crack-ing stick and alarm the snake. Distance gives safety and breathing room. When the snake senses you moving away, it remains coiled, but its tail stops rattling. As you walk around the snake at a nonthreatening distance, it uncoils and slithers away.

"Whew," is the only sound you make, as you move away from this present danger and head toward other possible dangers at home.

Exhausted from your fear, you walk slowly and think about the risks of going to unknown destinations. It is puzzling to you how you felt safe on your previous explorations away from home, but now you feel threatened by real and imagined situations. You wonder how you could almost miss the rattlesnake by being so focused on some imagined danger triggered by the footprint!

You are relieved when you reach the outskirts of the village. It is familiar and feels relatively safe at the moment, although people still will not look at you. You conclude it is never completely safe, even when it appears everything is fine. There are always known and unknown dangers.

Chapter 14 Commentary
It Is Never Completely Safe

Magnetic Pull of the Familiar

In seeking to find our own way, our fear of known and unknown dangers is at times stronger than our courage to leave the perceived safety and comfort of the familiar. We may venture out briefly but return "home" when things get difficult.

Without a disciplined, concerted effort to break away and the tools to manage fear and danger, we will always be tempted to go back to the familiar because we know how to deal with it. For this reason, most people never truly "leave home" to find their own way. However, it is an illusion that we are entirely safe at home in the familiar.

Dangers of Remaining in the Familiar

There is real danger in the magnetic pull of the familiar, because it lulls us to sleep. When we resign ourselves to the familiar, we do not live our own life. We go along with things that are not true for us and may remain in a toxic situation. We lie to ourselves. We do not speak up. We live in fear of making a mistake and being punished or excluded. We are anxious that we will not be taken care of. We are depressed because we are doing things we are told to do but have no interest in doing. We come to the dreadful conclusion that "this is all there is."

Questions to Consider

- *What danger exists for you in your present situation?*

- *If the danger is not obvious, do you recognize a feeling of being "ill at ease" about something or a sense that "It's not entirely safe" in a particular setting?*

- *What is your response to this sense of danger?*

- *Are you taking action to find greater safety?*

- *Does your fear of the unknown keep you doing the same thing day after day and stop you from trying something new?*

CHAPTER 15

Relaxation

While your external environment now feels safer, you notice that you still feel tense and alarmed inside. Instead of going directly into the village, you decide to pause to regain your composure.

Instinctively you move to a quiet, secluded place near a stream. You remember that you can soothe yourself by listening to your surroundings and that the more acutely you listen, the more present you become.

You sit comfortably on the bank of the stream with your feet planted on the ground near the water and you begin to sense your breath. The air is moist and cool as you inhale through your nose and warm as you exhale through your mouth.

You notice that your body begins to relax and you feel less alarmed as you deliberately let go of each breath of air. You feel encouraged that you can deepen your sense of relaxation by continuing to pay attention to your exhale as you release the tension from your body.

With a long, complete exhale you then imagine your scalp relaxing and the hair on your head and neck smoothing down. Your ears also relax and you now listen without straining or tension. When you release your jaw, allowing your mouth to open slightly, you notice your face softens. As your eyes close with your next exhale, your awareness turns inward. You hear the sound of your exhale through your open mouth.

You silently express your experience in words, "I am relaxing with each exhale." You then notice that your shoulders come down. With your next exhale, you let go of tension from your shoulders, down your arms, and out through your hands. When you imagine putting your hands in soothing warm water, they become warm, and you drop deeper into a state of quiet relaxation. You allow your hands to open with palms up.

Your chest expands with each inhale of breath and your long, quiet exhale brings your awareness down from your neck and chest into your belly and hips. With each exhale, you allow your belly to relax more completely.

You can now feel how your buttocks meet the surface where you are sitting. As you stop pushing and surrender to the earth, your attention drops down into your knees and lower legs, with a long, gentle exhale through your open mouth.

You then express your experience with a silent thought of,

"I am," on each inhale of breath and an even softer, "relaxing," with each exhale. You continue this rhythmic pattern with every breath.

Eventually, each exhale allows a continued relaxation from the top of your head, through your body, and down through your solidly planted feet. By spreading your toes, you make better contact with the ground. With each exhale, you allow the tension and fear to drain down out of your body and into the earth. There is a peaceful smile on your face, as you feel more at home inside yourself.

You have now learned to relax and quiet yourself. This allows you to listen carefully for your inner truth and direction. Your words come easily now, "I can comfort myself through this process of relaxation." Then you speak a deeper supportive phrase, "I will do it myself when there is no one here to help me."

Chapter 15 Commentary
Relaxation

At this point in our story, you have experienced the relief of leaving the village where it felt dangerous to your well-being. Then you encountered new, unexpected dangers on your travels. You remain fearful, as you conclude it is never completely safe. You make a decision to return to the familiar, believing the village is your safest option for the moment. Since our story is about being self-reliant, the question arises, "How will I guide myself under these anxiety-provoking circumstances?"

Relaxation to Reduce Fear, Think Clearly, and Listen for Guidance

When we are anxious and fearful, we do not think clearly. Our brains click off in a panic, and we make decisions that are not well thought through. It is important to first reduce fear so we can then find our way by making informed decisions from a clear, relaxed state. Self-relaxation is an important skill to reduce fear and create a safe place inside ourselves where we can listen for guidance. Relaxation of the body is the foundation for building Emotional Self-Reliance.

Regular practice in a variety of situations is required to develop this ability to relax. Then, when there is a surprise situation or an ongoing conflict that creates fear and anxiety, we are able to enter into a more relaxed state where we can think clearly, rather than spiraling into greater fear and confusion.

Practice: Relaxing Your Body

Initially, it is best to practice in a safe, comfortable setting where success will come more easily. Later, when you have built some skills at achieving a state of relaxation and clarity, you can expand your practice to more challenging settings to become more prepared and confident. Ultimately, the goal is to know the relaxation process well enough that you are able to do it independently at any moment. Begin your practice now. Take your time with each of the following steps:

1. *Find a comfortable place to sit.*

2. *Feel your feet making contact* with the ground or floor.

3. *Notice any sounds in the environment* to help you become present.

4. *Sense your breath,* as you inhale through your nose and exhale through your mouth.

5. *Read Chapter 15 of our story (again)* to be guided through the relaxation process that begins at your head and leads you down through your body to your feet. Consider making a recording of yourself reading the chapter out loud, allowing you to follow along later with eyes closed.
   - Start at the fifth paragraph: "With a long, complete exhale you then imagine your scalp relaxing . . ."
   - Read slowly and deliberately as you follow along.
   - Pause after each sentence to feel the effect in your body.

CHAPTER 16

Alert and Focused with Purpose

You stand up slowly and continue your walk toward the village. As you get closer, you struggle to stay connected to the peaceful and relaxed state you had just achieved.

You start to feel trapped between the dangers of leaving and the discomfort at home. Your uncertainty brings up fear, similar to what you experienced when you were terrorized by the footprint and confronted by the rattlesnake.

The old question of "What to do?" comes forward, but this time you respond out loud, "I intend to look within myself for answers."

You remember that when you encountered the rattle-snake, you did not run. Instead, you exhaled and gathered yourself together. This allowed your brain to move past the panic and assess the situation. This realization is a comfort to you, and it helps you to know this process can be used again to gather information before taking action.

You exhale fully and release tension from the top of your head down through your feet. You deliberately stand taller and engage your brain to consider the dangers in your current situation. First, there is the problem of returning to the village, where you are shunned for thinking independently. Then, there is the problem of your eventual departure to an unknown destination.

You remember that a plan of action helps to reduce fear. Then, activating the plan gives you direction and a new sense of purpose.

Your plan for entering the village now becomes clear as you verbalize it out loud to yourself: "Pay attention and trust your sense of danger. Stay inside yourself when others ignore you or shun you, by remembering your identity is based on your independent experiences. Do not be surprised or deflated if you are 'made wrong'—you know that this is to be expected, based on your previous interactions. And finally, always continue to learn from your own experiences and trust your conclusions in order to make progress, just as you did when you learned to throw rocks at a target."

You determine that the next problem to face will be the preparations necessary to survive on your own once you leave the village. To manage this overwhelming task, you make a supply list. You know which foods are easy to obtain and travel well, and you remember a container that you previously used to carry water. You decide it would also be good to bring some small items of value that could be traded for food and transportation on your journey. You realize you will need a sharp-edged tool for cutting and protection, and you can use that old leather bag you have to pack everything for easy travel.

As your list grows and your plans become more real, you begin to appreciate the challenges and dangers ahead of you. You remind yourself that once you are back in the village, you will need to eat healthy food and stay fit with exercise for the physical demands of the journey. You also know that you will need to seek quiet moments in peaceful locations to relax and remain centered on your goal. Now, with your current plan, your world feels a little more manageable.

Finally, you pick up your familiar rock and turn it over in your hand as you state, "I want my plans to fit my purpose, just as this rock fits in my hand."

You make your way closer to your village without drawing attention to yourself. As you take on an alert and focused attitude, while still remaining wary of danger, the image of a hunting coyote comes to mind.

As you enter the village, you realize that your organized preparation for leaving reduces your fear. Your confidence is growing with each step taken toward your journey of a lifetime.

Chapter 16 Commentary
Alert and Focused with Purpose

Plan for Known Danger

When we are returning to a known, dangerous situation involving interpersonal relationships, it is helpful to review what we already know and what we can expect will occur, based on past experiences. Then we can plan for what we believe to be the inevitable.

It is helpful to review our best options for taking care of ourselves when facing interpersonal conflict. By remaining alert and focused on our purpose in returning to the stressful situation, we can hopefully avoid losing our composure and our greater goal.

Questions to Consider

Consider a difficult interpersonal situation you are facing and ask yourself:

- *What is my goal in this situation?*

- *Who will I interact with?*

- *What do I know about this person and their qualities that I experience as dangerous to me?*

- *What can I expect from this person based on previous experiences?*

- *What personal reminders can I give myself in preparation for this encounter?*

- *Do any of the following personal reminders from our story fit for me?*

  ➤ Pay attention and trust your sense of danger.

  ➤ When others ignore you or shun you, stay connected to your own sense of identity, based on your independent experiences.

  ➤ Do not be surprised or deflated if you are made wrong—this could be expected, based on your previous interactions.

  ➤ Continue to learn from your own experiences and trust your conclusions in order to make progress.

CHAPTER 17

Things Do Not Always Go as Planned

Walking through the village toward your home, you suddenly and unexpectedly meet your father. He has been withdrawn and sullen since the night he confronted you about leaving. He challenges you now by asking sternly, "Where have you been? What are you doing?"

"Nowhere, nothing," you reply, feeling guilty.

He senses your discomfort and defensiveness, so he pushes harder, "You sure are out of breath and sweating from doing nothing."

Fearing his disapproval and possible anger, your body

reflects your sudden loss of confidence as your posture slumps. You silently gasp as if all the air has been sucked out of you.

Now he really puts you on the spot by asking, "Are you still thinking of leaving?" There is an awkward silence, so he presses on, "I hope you don't embarrass yourself and our family by doing something foolish."

Again, you find yourself sinking down in shame as you reply, "Okay, Father."

He finishes the exchange with one more blow before he walks off, "You had better talk to your mother—she has been looking for you."

You feel stunned. Your energy drains out of you and your head lowers. You look down—heart pounding, breath short, and unable to think—as if in shock. With your confidence erased, you feel lost as you walk slowly away.

You stumble along, looking for a quiet place to sit down where you will not be seen. A grove of trees welcomes you to sit on a large rock near a pond. You begin to cry softly, and these thoughts come into your awareness. *What will become of me? I feel so alone and unloved.* That old feeling that you must have done something terribly wrong comes back to you.

You feel young and vulnerable, as you realize how much you depend on others for emotional support. Parents, relatives, and the villagers have provided you with love, validation, and guidance up to this point.

You have prepared a list of things for your physical survival on your journey, and you have developed mental strategies for challenging situations. However, you now realize how difficult it is to support yourself emotionally when you feel lost, confused, made wrong, and unloved.

Now what do you do?

Chapter 17 Commentary
Things Do Not Always Go as Planned

Surprise Challenges

Although we may learn to plan and prepare ourselves for known dangers and challenges, we cannot possibly anticipate every challenging situation that could arise. There are always surprises along the way that can throw us off course or force us to regroup and possibly change direction. There is rarely a straight path to our goal, despite our best planning and efforts.

Personal Attack

We are usually not prepared for a surprise personal attack. When we are caught off guard and respond with defensiveness, fear, or awkward silence, the attack often intensifies and feels relentless. This onslaught can leave us feeling beaten down and stunned, with our confidence erased.

Personal Manipulation

An attack might come as an obvious confrontation but it can also occur through subtle manipulation. It can be disguised as a simple question, concern, expression of love, or complaint of hurt feelings. Yet each move this other person makes is calculated to get us back in line by discrediting what we are doing.

One simple comment or look can knock us down by planting a seed of doubt—causing us to question ourselves. Often this subtle kind of manipulation is the most dangerous, because we become confused by the appearance of care, concern, or hurt on the part of the other person. We can also feel threatened by the possible disapproval and loss of connection.

Loss of Emotional Support

People in our daily lives become accustomed to dealing with us in predictable ways. As we begin to change, this brings up uncertainty for them and they feel threatened. Perhaps we previously said, "yes" to their requests. Now we say, "I have other plans." They begin to experience their loss of control over us. They are then fearful and resist our changes by becoming critical of our ideas, disappointed in our actions, and angry at our defiance.

When it is a family member or other loved one who attacks, critically questions, or attempts to manipulate us, the resulting feelings of being unloved and unsupported can easily weaken us. We often then regress to a younger, more vulnerable state of emotional dependence.

So be prepared: *When you start living your own life, it may be one of the most unpopular things you will ever do.*

Questions to Consider

- *How do you support yourself emotionally when you feel alone, lost, confused, made wrong, and unloved?*

CHAPTER 18

Recovery

You sit still near the pond and exhale softly to gather your wits about you. You remember that listening to the surrounding sounds keeps you present. You relax and let go with your exhale, so your discomfort drains down into the earth through your belly, hips, legs, and feet.

Starting to bring yourself back to the present, you utter the words, "Now, wait a minute, I don't want to lose myself because of my father's opinion of me." Then you exhale more deeply to release your fear.

You remember your original idea to leave the village was not welcomed by others. You also realize you have already started your journey by paying attention and trusting yourself. Along the way you have learned new skills and solved problems. You have encountered danger, and you have learned to manage your fear so that you can make good decisions.

You take a moment to sit up taller and this creates more space in your chest to breathe and consider your present situation.

You realize that others have helped you in your life, but as a young adult you have continued to grow and become more independent. You remember the baby birds from your dream that swallow whatever they are given. You know you have progressed beyond this early stage. You now feel how you are similar to a maturing, young bird that is testing its wings in preparation for flight.

You do not feel as confused and lost when you begin to feel right, instead of wrong, about your ideas. As you remember your vow, "I will do it myself," confidence begins to return. It seems that somehow this problem of feeling unloved can also be solved.

You start by stating, "I could learn to love myself just as I learned to throw a rock and hit a target." Without thinking, you reach for the rock that fits so well in your hand. It has begun to feel like a comfortable companion. Just by holding it, some of your doubts begin to fade.

As you stand up and stretch, you feel taller and more capable.

You acknowledge, "It is time to look for my mother." You know you can find her working in the kitchen, but on the way there, you make a small detour to pick up your leather bag. There is comfort in wearing the old familiar bag that fits your back so well, and it reminds you of your vow to leave the village. Your confidence is recovered as you return to your list of things to do.

Chapter 18 Commentary
Recovery

Critical Thinking

As described in our story, once we have softened our body and become present through the relaxation process, it is helpful to engage our brain in critical thinking as part of a process of recovery from a personal attack. Critical thinking examines the facts, challenges the conclusions of the other person, and examines their motivation. Through critical thinking, we address the question, "What makes them 'right' and me 'wrong'?"

Practice: Engaging Your Brain in Critical Thinking

1. *Pause:* The first step in critical thinking is to pause long enough to reexamine what just happened. "Now wait a minute . . ." is a helpful phrase.

2. *Define what happened:* For example, "When my father confronted me, I collapsed inside and became weak."

3. *Examine the facts:* "My father has been telling me what to do for many years, and I assumed he was correct. I have been dependent on him for physical and emotional support. I am afraid of his disapproval and anger. He makes me feel wrong about my own idea of leaving. He is concerned about the family's reputation and wants me to follow his directions."

4. *Challenge the other person's conclusion:* "What makes my father think he knows what is best for me? I am older now and have my own ideas. I have already experienced success on my own without his direction or approval. It's not my job to keep the family from feeling embarrassed."

5. *Challenge your own initial response:* "I don't want to lose my own sense of direction based on my father's opinion of me."

Practice: Recovering from Setbacks

It is helpful to develop a process of recovery that you can utilize to regain your focus and confidence when you feel knocked down from a personal attack, criticism, or other setback. Consider the following example:

Relax from head to toe.

Exhale fully to release fear and discomfort.

Choose to feel "right" instead of "wrong."

Open your chest and stand tall.

Vow to "Do it myself."

Engage your brain in critical thinking.

Review past successes.

Yodel to have a little fun as you continue on your way.

CHAPTER 19

Sadness and Loss

"Father said you were looking for me," is your cheerful greeting as you enter the house.

"Where have you been?" your mother asks.

"Just taking a walk," is your stiff reply.

"What are you doing with that old bag?" she inquires.

You had not expected this question, but you try to hold your own by stating, "I just wanted it to carry some of my things."

"I hope you are not thinking of leaving," she says, demonstrating how well she knows you. "You are needed here at home, and there is leadership opportunity for you in the village. Others still remember and respect the things you did before you expressed your crazy idea to leave," she says. "It is time you settle down, find a good mate, and have some children. That would really please me. People will soon forget your idea of leaving. What do you think?" she asks.

Without disclosing your plan, you find yourself turning partially toward the door, before shocking yourself by blurting out, "I am still thinking of leaving." While honestly speaking your intentions, your own blank face makes it seem as if some other person has just spoken. Inside your head there is a quiet thought, "Now I'm in trouble!"

Your mother turns slightly away and begins to cry silently. Her sadness softens something inside your heart, so you move closer to give her a hug. She responds by holding you and there is a familiar, solid connection of love.

"I worry about you and what you are thinking," your mother says. "Who will be there to love you and take care of you? Who will be here to take care of your father and me when we get old? Nobody ever leaves the village, and our traditions keep us together. You have spoken the unthinkable. Please reconsider and stay."

In response to your mother's appeal, you manage to squeeze, "I love you," out of your tightened throat before you walk quickly out the door.

You immediately walk away from the house, as you feel sadness welling up in your chest. You softly cry out, "I had no idea it would be so difficult to leave. I love my parents and my life here in the village. I know how to live here and I understand the rules. But, something inside me still wants to go. How will I make the right decisions for myself and still feel loved as I find my own way?"

Chapter 19 Commentary

Sadness and Loss

The Lure to Stay Is Powerful

We are often drawn back into old, familiar ways of living or relating, because they feel easier, more comfortable, and predictable. We can also feel lured back to the familiar by experiencing a loving connection and/or sense of responsibility for a loved one.

Rescuing Ourselves from the Lure of the Familiar

Often when we feel a strong pull to remain in a situation, relationship, or lifestyle that we have taken steps to leave, a truth or intention can rise up in us that we then blurt out without thinking. It is as if we are trying to rescue ourselves from sinking further into the quicksand of the familiar that no longer serves us. We often feel shocked after we have impulsively revealed ourselves, and there is the urge to immediately get away without discussing the details. This is when we take the exit.

Questions to Consider

Think of a time when you made a decision and then started to doubt yourself based on a conversation with someone you cared about. You then found yourself being tempted to remain in an old familiar pattern.

- *Was there some part of you that blurted out a conclusion or comment that made it uncomfortable to stay and continue the conversation?*

- *Did you take a quick exit that rescued you from getting pulled back into the old pattern?*

- *Or did you stay and engage in a way that sabotaged your original decision?*

Appreciate that there is an impulsive part of you that can sabotage your best intentions and another impulsive part that can rescue you.

Sadness and Loss
In leaving, there will be sadness at the loss of the familiar, loving connection with others. At this stage, we do not know how we will support ourselves emotionally on our journey. We have had plenty of instruction and training to stay and no guidelines about how to leave. We feel how difficult it is to leave and do something different.

CHAPTER 20

Loving Yourself

You feel young, fragile, and shaken from the recent interactions with your parents. You look for a secluded place in nature to be alone and hide your face. Lying down under a shady tree, you begin to sob uncontrollably, like a child who is feeling alone and lost. Eventually, you find the words to ask out loud, "What will I do on my journey when there is no one there to love me and support me?"

Your crying subsides after you have clearly stated what you are upset about, even though you have no solution. You gather your wits about you by reviewing what helped you before when you lost your confidence, felt confused, or feared the unknown. You know that time alone in nature, relaxation, listening, and being present are important tools for recovery. When you are present, you are able to learn something new from your experiences that can help you move forward.

You take a moment to relax with long, slow exhales, as you listen to the sounds in nature around you. As you become present and notice your surroundings, you realize you are resting near the place where your grandfather is buried. A surge of warmth fills your chest, as you remember your grandfather with fondness and feel how much you love him.

You close your eyes and recall a special moment together when you were held on his lap as a child, while playing with some old toys he had saved and passed on to you. With this memory, you feel young and loved, as if you are still that child held so comfortably and securely.

As you lie there imagining the loving connection with your grandfather, you bring your hands to rest on your upper chest. Your breathing slows with soft, deep exhales, and your hands rise and fall on your chest with each breath.

When you pause briefly between the full, deep exhale and the next inhale, you spontaneously imagine an open window that you can travel through to experience a deeper sense of relaxation and peace. You imagine going through this window and, as you do, you let go to the moment and find yourself connecting more deeply with your body sensations and feelings.

You feel your heart expanding with love for your grandfather. You whisper, "I love you, Grandfather," as though he is right there with you. When you speak these words, you remember many more experiences with him of feeling this loving connection.

As your heart continues to open with love for your grandfather, you begin to think of other people in your life whom you love in the same openhearted manner. You take a moment to recall a pleasant experience with each person and, as you connect to this loving feeling again, you say, "I love you," followed by their name. With every person you love in this manner, your heart expands and warms your chest.

You allow this warm, open sensation in your heart to extend through your arms and into your hands. Now you can feel the warmth of your hands on your chest, as if you are being held in a secure and loving way. You wonder, "Is there anyone else I can add to this list of people I love?"

You pause briefly and then whisper once more, "I love you," and then you spontaneously add your own name. You feel the warmth of your hands connecting to your chest as you take in this new feeling of love for yourself. You soak up the warmth like a pleasant bath. Generating and then receiving this warm, heartfelt sense of love for yourself feels new, nourishing and healing.

Like an infant satisfied from nursing, you slowly open your eyes with your heart full of warm love that was generated through your own imagination! You are astonished to realize that you can intentionally provide for yourself the feeling of love that you previously believed only came from others.

You notice how different you feel! You came to this resting place with heavy sadness in your heart, and now your heart feels open, light, and full of love.

Before, you felt young, vulnerable, and dependent on others for love and guidance. Now, you feel older, independent, and more capable, knowing you can provide love for yourself. You feel transformed as you conclude, "When there is no one else there to love and support me, I will generate love toward myself through opening my own heart."

You repeat several times from your heart, "I love you," followed by your name. Slowly and with certainty, you begin to feel more confident in yourself as you affirm, "I can do this. I will use this process of 'loving myself' as the first step to support myself emotionally and guide the decisions I make on this journey." There is a real, undeniable feeling of joy, excitement, and energy in your chest that indicates you are on the right path.

Chapter 20 Commentary
Loving Yourself

*Step 1: Loving yourself is a heartfelt feeling
first generated and then received by you.*

External Source of Love

We are trained from our early experiences to look for love from outside sources. It is a wonderful experience when a supportive source of love is available. However, everyone who loves us fails us at some point. They may have a change of heart, grow tired, or be too busy to sustain the love we require in any given moment. We eventually must say "goodbye" to all those who love us because of departure or death. In the end, an external source of love is transitional, ever-changing, unreliable, and beyond our control.

Furthermore, in our attempts to secure love from others, we often confuse attention or approval with love. We believe we are loved when we are admired, praised, smiled at, or just plain noticed. In this precarious scenario, some might die wondering, "Was I ever loved at all?"

Internal Source of Love

In looking to be loved by others, we have lost sight of a more reliable source of love that is experienced when we love in an active way from our own heart. We first experience this internal source of love as a warm, heartfelt feeling that wells up in our chest when we love someone else—perhaps a parent, a grandparent, a lover, a friend, or a pet. It is an undeniable sensation in our heart. With intention and practice, we can learn to apply toward ourselves this self-generated feeling of love.

Transformative Process

By learning to generate our own source of love, we are transformed into independent, self-directed adults. We do not need to be so worried about whether people love us or approve of us. We are doing what we want, we love others, we love ourselves, and we make decisions based on the love we feel in our own heart.

From an External Source of Love	To an Internal Source of Love
Action	**Action**
1. *Look for love* from others.	1. *Generate love* in your own heart.
2. *Ask, "Do you love me?"*	2. *Ask, "Who and what do I love?"*
Outcome	**Outcome**
1. *Feel young,* vulnerable, dependent on others for love.	1. *Feel more mature,* capable, and emotionally self-reliant.
2. *Become lost,* weak, and indecisive, assuming others have the answers.	2. *Become self-directed* with an open heart as your guide.
3. *Feel heavy sadness and loss* when external love is not available.	3. *Feel energized and lighthearted* by generating your own source of love.

Step 1 Practice: Loving Yourself

Upon completion of "The Journey,"
you will find a guided practice for Step 1.

CHAPTER 21

Imagining the Future

Feeling supported and comforted by the love in your own heart, you get up and bring your attention back to your list of supplies for your journey.

You immediately begin the process of gathering food, tools, and clothing, which you pack carefully in your travel bag. You realize you will need to find a safe place to hide your supplies until you are ready to leave on your final journey. You decide it is best to take them with you the next day when you go on another exploratory trip. Your plan is to stash them on the forbidden side of the mountain, where no one from the village will find them.

The next day you take your supplies and go back up the mountain toward the place you left so abruptly when you discovered the footprints.

You walk easily now with energized steps. You hold your head high and your eyes are focused on the scenery in front of you. As you move on, your breathing deepens and every exhale sends renewed energy down through your legs.

With each step, your feet solidly contact the ground. You then push off with your toes to propel your body forward. You walk in a determined manner. You are on a mission and your focus is sharp. It comes to you that this feeling of energetic determination is what you want during your final departure from the village.

You begin to daydream of your ideal send-off with friends, family, and village leaders. What you hope for is encouragement, a vote of confidence in your decision, and well wishes from everyone.

As your pace quickens, you begin to feel a boost in your general well-being from your imaginary send-off. That kind of support would make your leaving much easier.

And then there is reality. Not one person thinks your idea of leaving is good. Even your mother has said it is "unthinkable." People have shunned you and turned away from you.

Your walking begins to slow significantly now, as you think about the reality of secretly leaving the village, all alone and unsupported. Your fear and hesitancy have returned and they drag on your energy and slow your movement. You wonder how you can possibly make this move all by yourself and where you will find support.

These thoughts bring you back to your commitment to "Do it myself." You then remember what you did when you were faced with other challenges in your travels.

You stop walking and pause briefly. "Now, wait a minute," you say out loud, "let me think about how I can solve this. I have good, original ideas, and I can teach myself new skills by paying attention and making corrections. I am also learning to trust my experience more, and I can make plans that energize me into action."

You reach for your rock and hold it. "I have learned that I can comfort myself," you say, "and, most important, I am learning to love myself as I love others." To affirm your resolve, you speak your name out loud, and with your whole heart you add, "I love you."

By redirecting your thoughts, you have reclaimed yourself and feel confident again in your capacity to support yourself and solve problems that arise. You feel relief as you exhale and begin walking again.

Chapter 21 Commentary
Imagining the Future

This part of our story contrasts the feelings and energy levels that exist when we are focused on the present plans for the day versus those that arise when we daydream too far ahead about possible, unsolved problems in the future.

Confidence and Determination
Versus Fear and Hesitancy

We often have a tendency to get too far ahead of ourselves. When we do, we can usually come up with events or situations for which we do not have answers. It is easy to leave a confident and determined state and enter one of fear and hesitancy by focusing on an uncertain future. It can then be extremely challenging to shift back from fear and hesitancy to confidence and determination. We can become so entangled in thinking about this future, unsolved problem that we do not take the immediate action we are capable of taking *today*.

Practice: Shifting from Fear and Hesitancy to
Confidence and Determination

When we are full of ourselves and get knocked down by events or our own fears, how do we pick ourselves up to begin again? This is a difficult task. It takes a disciplined effort of attention and action to return to a state of confidence and determination. The following choices can be helpful:

1. *Redirect your thoughts and attention.*
   - Review skills and recent successes to reconnect to an experience of confidence.
   - Return to your heartfelt feelings of love for yourself for support.
   - Recall your present task for the day to narrow your focus to something tangible and achievable.
   - Recommit to "Do it myself" to inspire a sense of determination.

2. *Apply yourself to the immediate task.* Focus on what is in front of you with an attitude of confidence that completing this task will lead you in the right direction. You do not need to know all the details or even the final destination, just take the next step!

3. *Be patient with yourself.* Shifting from fear and hesitancy back to confidence and determination can be challenging and will take time.

4. *Acknowledge any progress.* Celebrate success along the way—however small.

CHAPTER 22

Wanting the Best for Yourself

Finding your way up the mountain toward the other side, you continue with your thoughts about your final departure from the village. "Okay, what do I really want from others in my ideal departure, and how can I give this to myself?"

You decide to apply your first step of Emotional Self-Reliance to help solve this question.

From your heart, you speak out loud, "I love you" and then say your name. When you do this, you instantly feel the next supportive statement to be, "and I want only the best for you."

When you repeat, "I love you and I want only the best for you," you are flooded with hope and a feeling of support. So, you say it again, "I love you and I want only the best for you."

You feel how much you hunger for such emotional support, as you make decisions and take important steps in your life. It is a relief to know that you can begin to provide this support for yourself through the heartfelt attitude of loving yourself and wanting only the best for yourself. You recognize that you have discovered your second step of Emotional Self-Reliance.

You stop walking, look around, and listen, so that you can remember this place and this moment. Warmth wells up in your chest, and there are tears of recognition, as you say, "This is it! Even when everyone in the village turns against me, I can generate my own reliable source of love and an attitude of wanting only the best for myself."

As you continue your walk, you feel a growing sense of self-support and trust in your own resilience. You also find that your fear is reduced. You now know from experience that you can be afraid and regain your courage. You can feel knocked down by events or the opinions of others and pick yourself up. You are learning to solve things as they come up, and your sense of independence is growing.

You feel a stronger sense of self-reliance and confidence, and it energizes your strides away from the village. You continue over the top of the ridge to follow the stream down the far side of the mountain to search for the mysterious footprints. Any thoughts of real or imagined danger seem smaller, as you feel bigger and more capable.

Your breathing becomes full and deep when you repeat, "I love you," with each inhale and, "I want only the best for you," with each exhale. As you rely on yourself for support and guidance, you feel joy as each step takes you farther away from the village and into new territory.

Chapter 22 Commentary
Wanting the Best for Yourself

Step 2: Wanting the best for yourself is an attitude of support and encouragement similar to what might come from a helpful parent, teacher, friend, or guide.

Support and Encouragement from Others

Often we receive encouragement and well wishes from others at moments of opportunity and success or when we have an important decision to make. We may also receive this kind of support when we have a problem to solve or when facing a challenge, such as battling an illness or dealing with loss. When we are on the receiving end of such care and good wishes, we do not feel so alone in what we are going through and we often feel encouraged.

Additionally, others often supply advice about what they think is the best decision, plan, or direction for us. Certainly there are moments in our lives when someone offers exactly what we need at just the right time and it fits. However, even with our best interest at heart, others often have a difficult time consistently discerning what is truly best for us.

Support and Encouragement from Ourselves

"What do I really want from others . . . and how can I give this to myself?" This is the essential question at the heart of our story. When we learn to provide for ourselves what we are looking for from others, we feel empowered. We learn to give ourselves not only what we need in the moment,

but also what we may have needed previously. This then becomes a healing process as we "re-parent" ourselves.

We can begin this process by looking within ourselves to find a steady, reliable source of love (Step 1). Then, we can develop an attitude of wanting only the best for ourselves (Step 2).

Step 2 Practice:
Wanting Only the Best for Yourself

Upon completion of "The Journey,"
you will find a guided practice for Step 2.

CHAPTER 23

From Fear to Curiosity

You are alert and your senses are keen, as you easily find the footprints made by the unknown person on the forbidden side of the mountain. As you follow the trail left by the stranger, you notice that instead of fear, you now feel curiosity and heightened awareness of the present.

Occasionally, you have a worrisome thought of what to do if you encounter this stranger, but you bring yourself back to the task of staying alert and following the footprints. You intentionally remain relaxed and focused as you listen carefully to your surroundings and breathe with soft, deep exhales.

The landscape changes as you follow the small stream down the ridge. You notice that the stream is increasing in size and the vegetation on the surrounding hillsides is thick and lush with a healthy, green color. You temporarily lose the trail of footprints, until you think to look on the opposite bank to see that the stranger has waded across to the other side. Solving this puzzle increases your confidence.

As you continue downstream, the air is fresh with moisture and, as you inhale more deeply, you feel energized. You notice that the air has a distinct scent that is unfamiliar and yet invigorating. At times, when you go around a bend in the stream, you can detect a distant, rhythmic sound, similar to an open breath coming from the back of the throat.

This new scent in the air and the new distinct sound create a test for you to stay present, alert, and curious without allowing your fear-driven imagination to create unknown dangers. You have a growing sense of anticipation and excitement. You feel fully alive.

Chapter 23 Commentary
From Fear to Curiosity

Shifting from Fear to Curiosity

Out of fear, we anticipate something bad will happen. We often pull back and stop ourselves. With curiosity, we step forward thinking, *Let's see what happens next.* We stay present and alert without imagining catastrophes based on fear.

Increased experience and confidence allow us to approach a previously fearful situation with curiosity. Intentionally changing our attitude can also create this shift from fear to curiosity. Making this shift inside us is crucial to moving forward.

Practice: Being Curious

Welcome the day. Make an intentional experiment to stay alert, curious, and present with an attitude that "something interesting could happen."

CHAPTER 24

Discovering the Treasure

When you reach a small break in the foliage, you catch a glimpse of the prize that has been waiting for you. Quickly making your way to a clearing, you see that the river flattens out into a broad, shallow lagoon that flows past a sandy shore and into . . . a vast body of water!

You discover the sound you had been hearing is the seemingly endless body of water driving rhythmic waves that pour onto the gentle shore. The sight and the salty smell take your breath away. As you feel an enlivened sense of self in your heart, you spontaneously bring your hands to your upper chest.

"I can't believe the beauty!" you exclaim out loud. "I have never seen anything like it!"

You are overwhelmed with tears of joy, as you take in the beauty of the stream flowing into your newly discovered sea. It feels as if somewhere inside yourself, you have always known of this undiscovered treasure. You begin to understand that your original dream of leaving the village was driven by your courage and internal guidance to get you to this point. You cannot help but wonder if listening to your own counsel could bring you here, then what else might you discover?

You follow the stranger's footprints down to the broad shoreline where they have been erased by the waves. Your clues to the whereabouts of the unknown stranger have now disappeared.

Even though you are exhilarated from your discovery of the sea, the day is late and you quickly remove the food and other supplies from your leather bag and hide them in the shallow nook of a nearby tree. You leave immediately for the journey back to the village.

Chapter 24 Commentary
Discovering the Treasure

The Central Core of Our Experience
The chest area is a vital part of our body. In response to our experiences, we may open and expand or tighten and protect this area. When we are deeply touched by something, we can feel an opening in our heart and a greater sense of aliveness. Our hands may naturally come to our upper chest in response to such a powerful, moving experience. Additionally, when we have something important to say with confidence, we often straighten up and touch our chest as we speak. In contrast, when someone is shaming us or we lack confidence, we tend to tilt our head down and roll our shoulders forward to protect our heart.

The Real Treasure of Our Journey
When our heart expands and we are overwhelmed with tears of joy, we have discovered the real treasure inside. We feel alive and are connected to a larger sense of purpose. When this happens, we cannot help but wonder, "What else might I discover?" This sense of hope carries us forward on our journey. With curiosity, courage, and the internal guidance from our own heart, we may continue to make new discoveries that open our heart.

Questions to Consider

- *Think of something significant you have worked hard to accomplish and notice the progress you have made. Can you feel your chest open and expand with joy or excitement?*

- *Then consider . . . If you have been able to accomplish this, then what else might you discover when you apply your intention and sustained effort?*

- *Have you discovered something on your life's journey that gave you the feeling that you always knew it was there for you to discover?*

CHAPTER 25

The Poisonous Attack

While walking back to the village, you reflect on how you disobeyed the unspoken rules by announcing your idea to leave. Then, you followed your developing plans, which led you to discover a world unknown to your people.

You want to tell everyone about your incredible discovery, but your exploration violated a village taboo. You have already felt the shame and isolation of speaking out and besides, who would believe you?

What will help you decide if you are going to share this discovery with others? You remember your new steps of Emotional Self-Reliance: "I love you and want only the best for you." These steps have provided you with support and helped you listen to your own guidance, but at this moment they do not help you to clearly resolve the question of whether or not to share your discovery.

You are lost in your thoughts as you enter a dark, brushy area just outside the village that is full of shadows, vines, and dank-smelling undergrowth.

"What are doing you here?" a voice demands. It is the voice of your grandmother, which is so full of interrogation, that it jolts you back to the present.

You feel yourself jump as if you were ambushed. Your heart immediately begins to race as you sense danger. Your throat becomes tight and dry, and your voice cracks like an adolescent as you answer curtly, "Just walking."

You have never felt safe around your grandmother, and she is the last person you want to meet in this secluded area. For some reason, she represents your darkest fears of being discovered, the bite of disapproval, and being made to feel wrong about your own thoughts.

"You look as if you are up to some mischief," she challenges, as if she can discern your intentions.

Now you experience your vulnerability and smallness. She clearly has the upper hand and enjoys that position.

There is a dangerous, flashing glint in her eye. She rushes in as if she smells blood. You read her intent. This is not a moment of compassion and there is no hint of safety. The air is being sucked out of you as she speaks.

"I hear you are still thinking of disobeying the rules by leaving." Then she draws from her darkest powers to slam home the near-fatal blow, "How could you be so selfish to think only of yourself?"

She notices the paleness in your face and your inability to speak. She moves in closer to finish you off with a voice intended to ensure control over your decisions.

"Think of your family first, or you will find yourself all alone without support." Then she reveals how cruel she can be as she issues her threat, "If you choose to embarrass the family by continuing with your plans to leave, I will never speak to you again! It is up to you." With that, she turns and demonstrates her threat by leaving abruptly.

You watch her disappear into the shadows.

Chapter 25 Commentary
The Poisonous Attack

A Poisonous Person

Many of us have a person in our lives who is poisonous to our well-being. When in contact with this person, we easily end up feeling disrespected, negated, beaten down, violated, controlled, or harmed in some other way. The interaction affects our system so strongly that in an instant we can lose our confidence and sense of direction as we collapse into a younger, weaker, and more vulnerable state. It may only take a look, a comment, or a body gesture from this person to knock us down.

Even when we understand what this person can do to us, and we prepare ourselves with strategies to stay safe, they often surprise us with a new tactic and once again we have lost our footing.

Vulnerability to a Poisonous Attack

What makes us so vulnerable to a poisonous attack by a particular person?

- *Having a history of repeated, unsuccessful interactions:* We easily fall back into an old, familiar pattern.

- *Being fearful and defensive:* It is like dealing with a bully. We are defeated before anything has even happened because we are afraid of them and try to avoid them. We are more hesitant and pulled back in a defensive position, and therefore more vulnerable to their poison.

- *Being lost in thought:* We are not as present to assess our immediate environment and even less prepared to respond to surprises. We can therefore be "ambushed" more easily.

Questions to Consider

Think of a person you know who is controlling, enjoys having the upper hand, and can successfully belittle you. Interactions with this person leave you feeling young, weak, and vulnerable. You then lack the clarity and confidence to speak up for yourself.

- *What is your relationship to this person? Are they a friend, parent, teacher, spouse, coworker, or employer?*

- *What are the characteristics and actions of this person that make them dangerous or poisonous to you?*

- *What are you doing that makes you so vulnerable to their poisonous attack?*

- *What are some ways you limit your own strength and power around this person?*

- *What would you include in a personalized self-defense program to build strength, power, and confidence that you can successfully deal with this person?*

Standing Up for Yourself

The venom of your grandmother's words leaves you staggering and collapsed inside, as if the wind has been knocked out of you. Her intent to control is completely effective. You feel as if your confidence and sense of being a capable adult have been destroyed. You feel caught between a childlike sense of shame and a burning rage in your belly that is ready to explode. You feel like you cannot breathe.

Once your grandmother is gone, all you can think is, "I hate you!" Then your rage boils over and you scream out, "You evil witch! It has never been safe around you. I know who you are from my experience of you. You are the selfish, uncaring one . . . always demanding of others that they obey and serve you blindly. You are a cruel and controlling old woman, and your words make me want to spit. I will not swallow your poison, and I will not bow down to your wishes. I find you manipulative and unloving! My gut wants to retch and puke out your intent to control, because it makes me feel sick. Stay away from me!"

Your body trembles from your expressed rage, but you feel surprisingly better and more adult for coming to your own defense against her poisonous attack. You smile and begin to laugh at your own explosion of defiance. You are relieved that you have not buckled under from the weight of her repressive attitude. Despite what she said to you and your initial reaction, you realize this is the first time that she has not ultimately succeeded in controlling you.

"I will learn to trust myself and make decisions in my own best interest instead of bowing to the intimidating threats of others," you declare out loud.

You stand taller with an exhale of relief, "Well, I guess this experience answers my question of whether or not to tell anyone about my discoveries. I'm certainly not telling her! I think I had better keep my new discoveries to myself until I sense someone is interested in what I have to say and can be trusted with the information."

Chapter 26 Commentary
Standing Up for Yourself

Tolerating Mistreatment by Holding Anger Inside

As children, we often learn to "accept things the way they are" in response to being shamed or punished when we previously spoke out. Then as adults, we may continue to accept being treated in ways that are not good for us, as we hold our anger and resentments inside. We become long suffering, even though we have a deep sense of injustice.

Transformation through Initial Expression of Rage

As in many things, there comes a tipping point. The anger we have been carrying boils over as rage, and we finally come to our own defense as we blurt out the truth we have been holding inside. By standing up for ourselves in this spontaneous and uncensored way (whether or not the other person hears it), we are liberated from the old oppression that held us captive. We get out from under the original shame that controlled us. We then feel empowered.

Prior to this point, our self-advocating aggression had been missing. Now we resolve to respond to mistreatment differently. We are willing to fight for ourselves with the conviction, "I will not allow you to abuse me like this again."

Resolve to Respond Differently to Mistreatment

When we recognize the root of our anger, we can resolve to deal with the situation or person differently so that we are not left feeling abused or shamed. For example, in the story, your resolve is, "I will not swallow your poison, and

I will not bow down to your wishes." We might not be able to change the other person or the situation. Therefore, it is crucial that we come to a clear resolve that empowers us. When we do this, the personal attack against us is no longer effective.

Anger as Fuel for Productive Action
Once we achieve this new sense of empowerment and resolve that we *can* and *will* stand up for ourselves, we learn that we do not need to automatically "fire back" at people who attack us with their poisonous qualities. Rather, we can address the original situation with words and actions that are thoughtful, clear, and powerful without being delivered in rage. The key is that we are connected to our anger and use it as fuel for productive action. Consider the following applications of anger:

- Recognize the truth of our experience.

- Develop determination.

- Become more powerful.

- Resolve to respond to a situation or person differently.

- Speak up for ourselves.

- Confront abuse.

- Say a convincing "no."

- Fight for justice.

- Recover from shame.

Questions to Consider

• *Are you holding any anger inside in response to experiencing injustice or mistreatment?*

• *When you connect to your anger, can you verbalize the truth of your experience and then see the situation more clearly?*

• *With the energy and clarity from your anger, how do you resolve to respond differently to the situation so that you can stand up for yourself and feel more empowered (without being abusive or violent)?*

CHAPTER 27
Being Called Selfish

As you continue to walk your own path back to the village, you reflect on the actions of your grandmother to help you see more clearly who she is. You realize that she is concerned about her social status and does not want to feel embarrassed by decisions of other family members. She wants others to obey her so she can control them and maintain her position of power. She asserts control by threatening to disown others and clearly does not value the personal expression of ideas. You realize she is primarily concerned about herself without considering others.

You begin to wonder about the motivations of other people in the village who criticized and shamed you for your idea of leaving. In thinking about your father, you remember his attitude of disapproval. He admonished you not to do something that might embarrass him or the family. He apparently learned this form of control from his mother, whom you just experienced as the master of controlling others. Your father also appears to be thinking about his own status and well-being, while not considering what is best for you. He acts as if he holds the correct perspective for your life.

You then think of your mother who wants you to become a village leader, provide grandchildren for her pleasure, and be there to take care of her in old age. She also sees your idea only from her perspective when she calls it "unthinkable." She expresses concern that something bad will happen to you, while not considering that your idea of leaving might be good for you.

You then remember the village leaders who dismissed the meeting as soon as you expressed an idea that was different from what they expected or valued. They wanted to maintain their control over people to remain in power. In serving themselves and their own agenda, they did not consider how important it was for you to express your ideas.

As you think about the motivations of these different people who considered you selfish when you thought of leaving, you realize that each of them is actually serving themselves and not considering what is important to you!

You feel a burning irritation in your chest and anger in your belly as you exclaim, "Who are they to call me selfish? They are doing the same thing they accuse me of doing!"

You feel physically lighter inside and less oppressed after expressing your disgust at the hypocrisy of those who shamed you for your ideas.

As you walk into the village, you feel more relaxed. You notice a busy honeybee gathering pollen from the center of a yellow flower. The bee is covered with a dusting of pollen, as if it is bathing in this harvesting process. It moves quickly to another flower to gather as much pollen as it can before flying back to the hive, where the honey is made. It appears to be focused on what it needs to fulfill its immediate purpose, without considering the pollen that other bees might need. It makes you smile to think how this apparently selfish act is actually essential to the reproduction of the plant and to the survival of the bee colony!

Now you recall other examples in nature. You have noticed how the tallest tree reaches higher for the sun to support itself without adjusting its growth to allow precious sunlight to reach other trees or plants. Certainly it sinks its roots deeper for water and nutrients, which diminishes the supply for others.

You also remember watching birds fighting, defending their territory, and establishing a pecking order for eating, drinking, mating, and nest building. The pigs and goats in the village all know who eats first or commands the best shady spot to rest.

You conclude: "Certainly it is our nature to be self-serving, and this is often considered selfish by others." When you reflect on your own actions, you admit to yourself, "It's true I was only thinking of myself and did not consider how my idea would affect my family, my friends, or the village."

At first you are perplexed at your lack of consideration for others. Then you realize that because of your previously charmed life, where you were praised for your every thought and action, you automatically expected your original idea to be greeted with positive recognition and approval. You remember how you were shocked when everyone seemed to think you had a "bad idea."

You now know, from your life experiences, that people will have different reactions to your ideas. You can expect that some will respond positively and be encouraging when they agree with you. Others will react negatively and might try to make you feel wrong if they do not agree, feel considered, or anticipate any personal gain.

You finally understand why others called you selfish in such a shaming way. They wanted to stop you from pursuing your idea and influence you into going along with what *they* had determined was best.

Chapter 27 Commentary
Being Called Selfish

Calling Someone "Selfish" Is a Form of Control

It is generally agreed that being "selfish" is "bad." This message gets imprinted on us as children when we are told, "Don't be so selfish!" in response to proposing a new idea, expressing what we want, or taking action on an interest. It is such a powerful form of shaming and control that we often stop what we are thinking or doing. The other person's intent to control us is then effective.

We Stop Ourselves to Avoid Appearing Selfish

For many of us, we then spend our life containing our personal desires, out of the fear of appearing selfish. We may know the best direction for our life, but we have a difficult time pursuing it, because we cannot get past this fear. We may recognize clearly what is required to resolve a particular dilemma, but hesitate to act on our personal convictions.

Warning:
Emotional Self-Reliance May Be Considered "Selfish"

Be prepared—when you begin making choices based on loving yourself and wanting only the best for yourself, others may consider you "selfish." A helpful and playful attitude in response to being called selfish when we begin to change is, "Thank you. I've been working on that." We then no longer feel shame for doing something that is in our best interest.

Questions to Consider

- *Have you ever been called "selfish"? (If not, in what other ways have you been shamed or made to feel wrong?)*

- *What was your response?*

- *How did it impact your choices?*

- *What are you stopping yourself from doing now, out of the fear of being considered selfish?*

CHAPTER 28

Listening to Your Heart's Desire

Your thoughts continue as you arrive home, "What makes other people think they have the answer to what is best for me? Yes, as an infant they may have known what was best for my survival, but I have grown to have my own independent ideas of what is best for my life." You recognize that your ability to know what is best for you is evolving as you develop your skills of Emotional Self-Reliance.

As you move past your hurt from being made to feel wrong about your own thoughts and ideas, you begin to feel compassion for others who have ideas different from yours. You vow not to shame others or turn away from them because they see things differently. In finding your own way and determining what is best for you, you decide you will also consider the ideas of others.

As you make this promise to yourself, your heart begins to open and you remember your mother and the sweet embrace you shared with her. When you were growing up, she was there for you. She cared for you and you always felt her love. You also learned to open your own heart by loving her. This love for your mother, in addition to the love for your grandfather, helped you learn to love yourself.

Now you know it is important to consider your mother's desire for you and listen to her wisdom about what she thinks is best.

You decide to test how her ideas resonate with you by using your first two steps of Emotional Self-Reliance. You say to yourself, "I love you and want only the best for you; therefore . . . I will follow my mother's advice by staying in the village. I will get married, have children, become a leader, and take care of my parents in their old age."

As you say this, your body slumps and your head drops down. You experience no energy or excitement about this conclusion. You feel a weight of responsibility on your shoulders, as if this is something you are supposed to do instead of something you want to do.

Your loss of energy tells you this proposed decision is not in your best interest. You could still choose to please your mother out of love for her by staying, but then you wonder, "How will I develop my own sense of direction by living according to my mother's desires for me?" And you feel haunted with the thought, "I could serve her wishes, but in doing so never truly find and live out my own heart's desire."

When you pause to feel your heart's desire, the original idea of leaving comes back to you. As you consider this option, you stand taller, your chest expands, and your heart beats faster. You feel energy and excitement for the journey that awaits you. You are now certain this is the right choice for you.

You remember your earlier conclusion to become a picky eater to take in only the information that rings true for you. You decide that even when you consider others in your decision making, you will carefully discern what is the healthiest direction for your life. By listening for your joy, energy, and excitement, your heart tells you what is the best path for you.

Your third step of Emotional Self-Reliance now becomes obvious to you: "I will listen carefully to your heart's desire."

Immediately your hands come up to touch your upper chest as if you are holding and listening to your heart. You state, "I will learn to listen carefully to the dreams, whether possible or not, from my heart to understand my deepest longing."

Your original idea of leaving comes into your awareness again. You notice this heartfelt desire radiating from your chest as a lighter, self-directed energy. You breathe easily and feel relaxed. You are confident and energized about your decision to leave the village.

You repeat your three steps together: "I love you and want only the best for you," and then you say your name. After a brief pause you continue, "And I listen carefully to your heart's desire." You feel excitement and joy as you declare, "I will trust these steps to guide my life toward greater self-reliance."

As you continue with your preparations for leaving, there is a coordinated flow to your movements, and tasks are accomplished easily with little effort. For now, the conflict about being directed by others or yourself has been resolved, and there is a new and powerful sense of self-reliance. All aspects of your experience are now in harmony and directed toward your goal of leaving.

Of course, you know there are still problems to be solved and uncertainties will always be encountered, but your personal confidence has reached a new high.

It is easy for you to say, "I know my heart's desire based on love and wanting the best for myself. The excitement in my chest and ease of breathing tells me I am following my heart's desire and living in alignment with my true nature. As I listen and give to myself, I can heal those old wounds of being made to feel wrong, with my own love, compassion, and self-direction."

Chapter 28 Commentary
Listening to Your Heart's Desire

*Step 3: Listening carefully to your heart's desire is a choice
to find direction based on the guidance of your heart.*

Heart's Desire as an Internal Compass

When our heart's desire is recognized and applied to our
lives in a disciplined manner, it becomes an internal com-
pass that serves as our primary guide for decision making.
Step 3, in combination with Step 1 of loving ourselves,
and Step 2 of wanting the best for ourselves, helps us
evolve into emotionally self-reliant individuals.

Disconnection from Our Heart's Desire

Often our original heart's desire is to be recognized, held,
and loved in a supportive manner. When these conditions
are not met and instead we are ignored, unsupported, or
shamed, we close ourselves off with a protective armor of
shortened breath and tight muscles to hide our vital feelings
inside. Because we are busy defending ourselves, we stop
listening to our heart's desire. Remember, as well, that we
have been socialized to want certain repeated and adver-
tised values. In going along with the direction of others,
there is less conflict and this brings some relief. However,
we have lost the connection to our heart's desire. Oops!

Connecting to Our Heart's Desire

1. Process Past Trauma

We may experience pain and anger when we recognize how our desires were not listened to or supported in our early years. The best medicine to heal these old injuries includes being held and listened to today in a safe, secure way so we can relax, inquire, and begin saying out loud what happened to us. As we express our truth and feel met with love, support, understanding, and acceptance, our muscles relax and our protective shell of armor softens. When we are assured we will continue to be held securely, we feel safe to go deeper inside. Then, we can begin to feel our heart's desire once again.

A good friend or therapist can often "hold" us with just the right attention and understanding that allows us to open and process our past trauma. We can also learn to be this supportive person for ourselves by using our own hands to hold our heart in a loving way, while listening with acceptance to what emerges.

2. Hold Ourselves and Listen Inside

To "hold" ourselves, we can begin with the relaxation process, followed by the practices of Step 1: "I love you" and Step 2: "I want only the best for you." As our hands make warm contact with our chest and we generate an attitude of love, acceptance, and support, we can hold ourselves securely. We can then listen carefully for that still, small voice inside to express our heart's desire, which is Step 3.

3. Healing a Broken Heart

When we recognize and pursue our heart's desire, it heals our old wounds from previously desiring something that was negated or not allowed. Sadly, sometimes in life we lose the possibility of achieving or living out our heart's desire. This could be the result of illness, the departure or death of others, financial hardships, or other losses. We then experience a "broken heart," which is devastating. It may feel as if there is nothing left to live for. The only cure for this broken heart is to mourn our loss and open ourselves to the possibility of a new heart's desire. When we discover it, we feel hope and excitement that once again we can live our life based on the desires of our heart.

Step 3 Practice:
Listening Carefully to Your Heart's Desire

Upon completion of "The Journey,"
you will find a guided practice for Step 3.

CHAPTER 29

The Surprise Opportunity

The next day, you fill your bag with extra supplies to add to your growing inventory hidden by the sea. Your energized steps quickly take you away from the village, up toward the mountains, and over the ridge with ease. Since you know the way, you easily follow the small stream on the other side of the ridge, where it grows larger before spilling into the sea.

You immediately go check the supplies you hid in the nook of the tree and are shocked to notice that something is wrong. The clothes have not been touched, but the three loaves of freshly baked bread that you brought from the village are gone!

"Someone has been here," you whisper. Has someone from the village discovered you, or worse, has the unknown stranger been watching you? Your heart pounds with fear. Your breathing becomes shallow. Your brain feels numb and you cannot think clearly.

You then remember that you can calm yourself and be more present by breathing deeply and listening to your surroundings. You exhale and let go of the tension so that you can listen for your inner direction.

You step back to look around and calmly assess the situation. You quickly see that there are no crumbs or broken pieces . . . so the bread has not been eaten here but instead taken away.

Then you notice a package wrapped in large, fresh leaves in the tree above you! "It has to be a clue to what has happened here," you think to yourself. Your legs tremble as you climb the tree. You reach for the package and fumble to uncover the clue inside. What you find makes you gasp, "fish!"

Three freshly cleaned fish have been carefully wrapped in leaves and placed in the tree. Your mind whirls with confusion until it all makes sense. Someone discovered your stash of supplies, took your bread, and replaced it with fish, which were stored safely for your discovery.

"A trader!" you blurt out with excitement at all the new possibilities. You realize that a surprise loss of supplies that appeared threatening is actually a gift in disguise.

Your thoughts go quickly to formulate a plan. More bread for more fish could establish an ongoing trading relationship with this unknown stranger who has made a fair exchange. You then remember that events can change unexpectedly but, for the moment, you find yourself smiling at your good fortune.

"Better make the best use of this opportunity!" you state emphatically.

Chapter 29 Commentary
The Surprise Opportunity

Making Use of Opportunities

Life is unpredictable and the best plans are subject to change. If we remain rigidly fixed on our original plan, we may not notice a surprise opportunity right in front of us.

Practice: Responding to Surprises

When pursuing your heart's desire, it may be helpful to:

1. *View* surprises, disappointments, and losses as possible opportunities.

2. *Consider,* "How can I make the best of this situation?"

3. *Remain open* to new possibilities.

4. *Stay curious* and interested as you "roll with the punches."

5. *Be light on your feet* and willing to change direction to accomplish your goal.

CHAPTER 30

Supporting Your Heart's Desire

"But, what about the bread?" you ask out loud.

You realize that even though it was convenient, you cannot keep taking bread from the village supplies. At first it was appropriate to take some for your own use, but for your new trading venture, you do not want to be dependent on village resources. You remember that sometimes outside sources of support can be unreliable and often come with expectations.

You decide it is best to count on yourself and use your own energy and resources, whenever possible, to support your heart's desire.

Now you realize your fourth step of Emotional Self-Reliance, and you say it to yourself: "I support your heart's desire with my best resources."

You feel the power and personal responsibility of this statement. It is exciting to claim, "It is up to me to make this a successful trading venture. I will do it myself!"

A plan begins to take shape in your mind: *First, I'll bake the fish by wrapping them in broad, green leaves, placing them in an open pit of hot coals, and covering them with clean sand to keep them moist.*

Second, I'll divide the fish onto three attractive plates and add vegetables.

Third, I'll trade one plate for bread-making ingredients and supplies. I'll trade another plate for bread-baking instructions from a village baker. I'll present the last plate to my family for a special dinner before my final departure.

Fourth, I'll bake enough bread for the family dinner and for my next trade with the stranger.

You sense that implementing this plan will help you become the best supporter and biggest fan of your heart's desire. You do a quick check with your first three steps:

- Loving yourself.
- Wanting only the best for yourself.
- Listening carefully to your heart's desire.

You then add this new step:

- Supporting your heart's desire with your best resources.

The plan fits! You are filled with joy, excitement, and enthusiasm for the tasks that you have set forth for yourself. You know that with hard work and determination, this plan can succeed. Your confidence leads you to action.

You immediately unpack your bag and leave the additional supplies in the nook of the tree by the sea. You carefully pack the fish in your bag and walk directly back to the village.

Over the next several days, your plan unfolds smoothly. Even the special dinner with your family goes well, because you do not discuss your decision to leave. Instead, your focus during the meal is on your appreciation of everything your family has done out of love and care for you.

The dinner is your personal celebration of success with beautifully baked fish and the best brown loaves of bread your mother has ever tasted.

Because you have a good memory for danger, you keep a safe distance from your grandmother. You disarm her with special attention by always serving her portions first. While showing respect for her position in the family, you tell yourself silently, "I will serve her food, but I will not serve her authoritarian directives."

When asked about the meal, you tell your family, "I did it myself." Nobody catches your humor about "The Little Red Hen" phrase, since they have all forgotten the story and the lesson.

You do not mention leaving the nest, although you feel as if you are a young bird stretching your wings to catch each breeze as you eagerly lean farther over the edge in anticipation of your departure.

You are now certain of your intention to leave, so you gather your strength and determination in preparation for conquering the unknown trials ahead. You have finished your list of preparations, including baking the bread intended for trade with the stranger.

You will know when the time is right for your final departure. There will be just the right combination of possibility, planning, and confidence to lean forward enough that the breeze will catch under your wings and you will fly!

Chapter 30 Commentary
Supporting Your Heart's Desire

Step 4: Supporting your heart's desire with your best energy, power, and resources is an action to invest wisely in yourself.

A Great Benefactor

Some individuals are born with a great benefactor. They are provided for in a way that any request is honored and every wish fulfilled. The time, money, and resources are available to support any personal desire. They live the charmed life of a prince or princess. It is often our fantasy to have such a benefactor: "If only someone would love me (Step 1), want only the best for me (Step 2), see me clearly and listen to what I want (Step 3), and then support me to fulfill my heart's desire (Step 4) . . ."

However, to be emotionally self-reliant, we must learn to provide our own support for our heart's desires. We then evolve into our own best benefactor through directed effort and practice.

"Parenting" Ourselves

Parents of most species offer a great example in their consistent daily efforts to provide for their offspring so they can survive and prosper. It takes moment-to-moment monitoring of their young to notice what they want and then provide the required food, shelter, education, and encouragement to grow. Parent birds demonstrate constant and tireless activity in their busy flights for food in the care of their young. How can we "parent" ourselves in the same manner to support our heart's desire?

Investing in Ourselves

When we are emotionally self-reliant, we sustain ourselves with the power and resources to help achieve our goals. Can we see the desires of our heart clearly enough and then provide the continuing resources to support them to the best of our ability? When we see the worth of what we are doing, we can invest with confidence.

Step 4 Practice:
Supporting Your Heart's Desire
with Your Best Resources

Upon completion of "The Journey,"
you will find a guided practice for Step 4.

CHAPTER 31

The Free Gift

The next morning at early dawn, just as you have practiced, you leave your village to travel to your trading tree by the sea. Your bag is packed full. Although heavy, you carry it with ease as you slip past the usual markers on your trail. There is no doubt about your intention to establish a trading relationship with the unknown stranger.

You arrive at the trading tree full of hope and excitement. You open your bag to take out the bright cloth streamer that you made as a signal flag for trading.

"Something is wrong! Someone has been in my bag!" you gasp. You quickly go through your supplies and everything seems to be exactly as you packed it. Then you notice a small leather pouch that you have never seen before. You pick it up and open it with trembling hands.

"A piece of flint!" you shout out.

Holding the flint, you remember the time your father showed you how to make a fire by striking the flint against an iron stone to create sparks. Because flint is rare and hard to find, it is exactly what you need for your survival and ongoing adventure.

You are stunned. Who has secretly placed this special gift in your bag? You quickly look for a note and you find no clues.

Somebody knew of your immediate plans and did not report you or try to stop you. Even though no one spoke publicly in favor of you leaving, someone was quietly supportive of your original idea.

You begin to weep tears of joy, as you are overwhelmed by the circumstances of this surprise gift. You may be completely alone in your adventure, but some unknown person has seen you clearly and lends support for your dream.

This person has given you exactly what you need without you asking, and the spirit of how it was given will travel with you forever. This is the essence of a free gift.

You are deeply touched. You carefully return the stone to its leather pouch and place it in your bag next to your familiar rock that provides the reminder of knowing when things fit for you.

You bring your awareness back to the task at hand by climbing the tree and attaching your trade signal to the upper branches. You can feel more than ever that the timing is right and your departure is near.

Your raised flag is your welcome to this unknown trader. It has the combined symbols of bread and fish to communicate that you have discovered the fish and have more bread for an exchange.

This unknown stranger could not possibly know of your hopes and dreams, nor do you know their intentions.

Chapter 31 Commentary
The Free Gift

Unspoken Support

Even when no one speaks up publicly in support of our ideas, there might be (and often are) others quietly watching who secretly believe in us but are afraid to come forward to stand beside us in an act of support and encouragement. However, often when we have successfully accomplished our goal, many people are willing to stand beside us and join in the celebration.

Free Gift

Sometimes in life a free gift appears and we might not even know the source of the gift. It is considered "free" because there are no strings attached. It often arrives as a complete surprise—not tied to a birthday or any other occasion. We are not looking for it and we do not expect it, but it touches us deeply. The free gift might be an object, a smile, a comment, an experience, or a turn of events that ends up being exactly what we need. There is something that feels magical about its appearance at this particular time. Such a free gift is often life-changing and renews our belief that something good can happen.

Questions to Consider

• *Have you ever received a free gift?*

• *What was the context, and what impact did it have on you?*

CHAPTER 32

The Commitment to Yourself

You climb down from the signal tree to wait on the shore so that you are clearly visible from the sea and the surrounding mountains. Exhaling in an attempt to relax, your mind begins to turn, driven by anxiety and worry about an unknown outcome.

Your fear makes you long for a partner on the journey—someone who has taken a vow to stay with you and work for a common cause. Your loneliness and sense of fragility begins to weaken your resolve, as you wait for a response to your signal flag.

You feel tremendous uncertainty as you wonder, "How will I do this myself, without a partner?"

You state your wishes out loud, "I want someone to support me during my darkest hour when success seems impossible and defeat appears imminent. I want someone to be here for me when all others turn against me and refuse to help. I want someone to hold me and comfort me when I am tired and afraid. I want a best friend and partner by my side during difficulties and successes."

Your hands come back to your chest to reconnect with your heart's desire to leave. You turn again to your steps of Emotional Self-Reliance and you review them out loud; "I love you, want only the best for you, as I listen carefully to your heart's desire, and use my best resources to support your dreams."

After taking in this heartfelt support you have just generated for yourself, you feel comforted and know you are at exactly the right place.

You realize it is up to you to be your own best friend and partner in this situation. Your fifth step now comes to you: "I will stay with you in success and failure and keep this as a lifelong commitment."

You embrace this commitment, exhale deeply, and feel relief as you surrender to the present moment.

You consciously take responsibility by affirming: "I am here because I choose to be here to follow my heart's desire. I have trusted myself and developed courage through my own actions. I have directed myself here and done all I can, so now is the time to wait patiently."

You feel ready to count on your deepest sense of determined self-reliance.

Chapter 32 Commentary
The Commitment to Yourself

Step 5: Staying with yourself in success and failure is a lifelong commitment to:
1. *Love yourself.*
2. *Want only the best for yourself.*
3. *Listen carefully to your heart's desire.*
4. *Support your heart's desire with your best resources.*

Supportive Partnership

Step 5 is the supportive partnership we look for in others, similar to a marriage vow, business contract, or government guarantee. However, this outside support is not reliable because others come and go, promises are not kept, marriages fail, businesses go bankrupt, and governments change. To be emotionally self-reliant, we make a life-long commitment to support ourselves during success and failure.

Support during Success

We may be most vulnerable when we are achieving success, because on the back of success often comes failure or loss. During success, things are going our way and we feel invincible. It is a moment of great personal triumph. This is when we are most vulnerable because we ignore our own mortality, lose our sense of humility and compassion, and then forget to share the gifts we have received.

At times, our most difficult challenge is to experience the excitement of success without losing ourselves in the process. The successful moment passes too quickly and we come back to our fears of not being loved, cared for, held, listened to, and supported from a dependable source.

Support during Failure

Most successful people admit to making mistakes. However, they watch carefully to not repeat the same mistakes. In learning to be emotionally self-reliant, we can also make mistakes. We might try things that do not turn out to be in our best interest. We also might fail to achieve our goal, despite our best efforts and decisions. We might work really hard and do everything right, and it still doesn't work out. Thus the vow to continue our commitment to ourselves is crucial when life becomes difficult, mistakes are made, setbacks and losses occur, or goals are not achieved. This commitment includes being patient and willing to try again.

Step 5 Practice:
Staying with Yourself in Success and Failure

Upon completion of "The Journey,"
you will find a guided practice for Steps 1 through 5,
called The Five-Step Practice of Emotional Self-Reliance.

CHAPTER 33

Anticipation

You wait patiently in an alert, relaxed state, ready for a response to your signal flag high in the tree. You do not know where to look or what to listen for. You have no idea how the response will appear.

You calm your anxiety by knowing you have given yourself to this task with love, wanting only the best for yourself, listening carefully to your heart's desire, and committing yourself to following and supporting your heart's desire during success and failure. So you continue to wait.

The signal first appears as a floating dot far out at sea. The dot bounces up and down like a small duck paddling slowly toward the shore, appearing to come closer and then being driven back by the wind and waves. There is a distinct reaction inside your chest in response to this faint unknown signal. Excitement wells up in your heart, as you feel it beat stronger and faster.

You feel full of energy and expectations. "What is it? Who is it? Will they see and answer my signal of trade? Is there some unknown danger that I do not see because I am so focused on my plan for success?"

You remember how you almost stepped on the rattlesnake when you first fled in fear of the unknown footprints. "But then," you say quietly, "things have changed as fear has turned to excitement." Your focus and energy are now directed toward possibly meeting the owner of those initially fearful footprints.

As the dot on the sea comes closer, you can tell it is a floating wooden boat apparently directed toward your flag. You gather your loaves of bread and raise one loaf high above your head to signal your intention.

When you see a figure stand up on the wooden boat and lift a fish in his hand, your heart leaps into your throat and tears well up in your eyes.

"It's the trader!" you shout excitedly. "Now I must think clearly and make decisions in my best interest using my five steps to guide and support me."

The boat moves straight toward the shore where you are standing. You wait patiently and remain quiet, so as not to alarm your potential trading partner.

As the boat reaches the shore, you clearly see a man standing and controlling the direction of the vessel. You can also see a woman and two small children in the boat, sheltered from the sun and spray of the sea. The man and woman are dressed simply and appear to be unarmed.

You stay in your position with the bread in full view and wonder out loud, "Is this the moment I have been waiting for?"

Chapter 33 Commentary
Anticipation

"Is This the Moment I Have Been Waiting For?"
This exciting moment of opportunity in our story is a culmination of all the lessons and accomplishments we have achieved up to this point, including:

- Moving ahead on our own, even when others attempt to shame us.
- Using our body sensations and energy to guide us.
- Staying present by listening carefully and paying attention.
- Channeling anger into determination to accomplish a goal.
- Learning from experience and building confidence.
- Determining when ideas fit for us.
- Developing a new identity based on experience.
- Doing it ourselves, as told in "The Little Red Hen."
- Managing fear and assessing danger.
- Calming ourselves through the relaxation process.
- Remaining alert and focused with purpose.
- Staying focused on the immediate task.
- Being adaptable when things do not go as planned.
- Recovering from setbacks, sadness, and loss.
- Transforming fear to curiosity and then to excitement.
- Standing up for ourselves.
- Making the best of a surprise opportunity.
- Remaining open to the possibility that something good can happen.
- Making decisions and supporting ourselves with the Five Steps of Emotional Self-Reliance.

Questions to Consider

- *Which of the previously listed lessons have you started applying to your own life?*

- *What have you discovered or accomplished through the application of these lessons?*

CHAPTER 34

Taking the Plunge

You remind yourself to exhale and stay in the present as the stranger pulls the boat ashore and walks up the beach toward you. The man is about your size with large, work-worn hands. He carries a basket of fish and, as he approaches you, you look directly into his eyes as you extend your open hand to him. After a moment, he reaches out his hand in greeting.

"Hello," says the trader in an accent unknown to you.

As you shake hands, you realize this is more than an opportunity for trade! And you think to yourself again, "Is this the moment I have been waiting for?"

You say, "Hello" to the fisherman, and then continue,

"We could trade bread for fish again . . ." Then, with your heart pounding, you state your deeper heart's desire, "but, what I really want is a ride."

"That will cost you more than some loaves of bread!" he answers emphatically.

You are thrown off by his challenge, but you regain the intent of your offer and state, "I can work."

He laughs and says, "I don't know where you come from, but you do not look like a fisherman. What do you know about fishing?"

You remember to keep your wits about you, because these negotiations are crucial. You then reach back into your experiences and your brain clicks on.

"I know fish swim in large groups for protection, and they gather into tight easy-to-catch schools when threatened," you say.

The fisherman draws up his chin and nods his head in agreement, as his wife and children come closer to take a better look at you. You nod and smile at them and reassure yourself silently, "I like these people and trust my sense that they do not intend to harm me."

"That is still not enough to buy a ride," the man says.

The fisherman's reply sets you back momentarily. You can see that he drives a hard bargain for traveling with them. You feel the pressure of the situation because of your desire to leave.

The only way you know how to travel far away from the village is to go with them. You realize you must make an appealing offer in addition to bread, work, and knowledge of fish.

Without hesitation, you stand taller with your head level as you look directly at the fisherman and state clearly, "I can throw a rock to hit a target."

The fisherman and his wife howl with laughter.

"How does that catch fish?" the man asks. "Do you hit them with a rock?"

"Yes, I could do that," you say, laughing with them, "but that is not how I catch them. Let me show you a new way to fish."

You carefully select a rock from the beach that fits just right in your hand. "Pick a target for me to hit!" you tell the fisherman, knowing you have what it takes to silence his laughter.

He accepts the challenge, looks around, and points to a small clump of seaweed floating a good distance off the shore, "Hit that target. That is where the fish hide."

You smile because you know you have him hooked—all it will take now is to draw him in slowly and you can make an offer that he will accept. Remembering everything it has taken you to arrive at this moment, you exhale and lock your eyes on the target. "Here we go," you say.

You throw the rock just as you taught yourself by paying attention and learning from your experiences. Your confidence is up as you watch the rock arc high and fly directly to hit the seaweed with a splat.

The fisherman and his wife stop laughing, and their eyes are wide with amazement. The fisherman, however, is a man hardened by the sea and not easily impressed. "But how does that catch fish?" he asks.

"I get a strong line of cordage and tie one end to the

front of the boat," you say looking directly at him and smiling warmly. "On the other end of the cordage, I tie a rock and a baited hook. I throw the rock and bait exactly where you tell me the fish are hiding. When a fish grabs the bait, I hook him and pull him into the boat. Then I bait the same line and throw it out again at your direction. If you would like, I can teach you and your family to fish this way as well."

The fisherman is speechless. He looks at his wife and she nods her head in agreement. Then, as a gesture of welcome, she prepares some space on the boat for your travel bag.

You breathe a sigh of relief, as you take a last look back at the land where you were born and give thanks for all it has provided. In your own way, at this moment, you hold in your heart everyone who has ever held you, fed you, and loved you. At the same time, you are confident that the ongoing love, guidance, and support that you need are right there inside you.

Your easy step aboard the swaying boat opens the door to the journey of a lifetime.

Reflections

When you look back on your departure, you recall those first horrific days of being a fisherman . . . tossed about on the sea with nausea and vomiting as your only signpost of progress. Your sickness called into question your decision to leave home.

The journey was indeed difficult, and you were tempted many times to turn back to where it was once safe. But then you remembered how your own people turned on you when you started thinking for yourself. So, you continued on to find your own way.

You made choices in your best interest and supported yourself emotionally by using your Five Steps of Emotional Self-Reliance that made your departure possible.

You faced danger and used your wits to overcome the perils of the journey. You met others along the way who offered help and had information that was useful, but in the end you trusted your own counsel to make decisions.

You discovered through your interactions with others, that people eventually revealed who they really are—especially when you disagreed with them or made independent choices. You became determined to watch people closely and trust your experiences of them.

In your travels through foreign lands, you observed many different people and ways of life, but you learned that every group had something in common with your village: People were made to feel wrong for their independent thinking.

You had compassion for those who were shamed for their ideas and tried your best to listen and understand what it was like for them. This compassion for others helped to heal your own wounds of being made wrong and shamed.

When people asked how you were able to leave your village on your own, you shared with them your Five Steps of Emotional Self-Reliance.

Great success came to you, as you followed your heart's desire and made decisions with love and wanting the best for yourself.

One day, you decided to return to your village. The village had heard of your success, and you were welcomed home as a hero. People turned out to greet you and receive the gifts you brought from faraway places.

You felt great joy upon learning that your leaving made it possible for others to leave and follow their heart's desire.

People brought back new ideas to the village, so it could thrive instead of becoming stagnant.

You discovered that just like the honeybee gathering pollen, your so-called "selfish" actions also benefitted others.

Everywhere you went people gathered to acknowledge your accomplishments and then took credit by saying, "I always knew you could do it." You smiled and thanked them, but trusted what was true from your own experiences. You silently made a note in your journal:

I know I truly travel alone, because these people were not there for me when I sought support and guidance to find my way. They had their own plans for me that served them.

I learned to face my fears, tolerate the discomfort of feeling uncertain, and make choices in my best interest. I did it myself, and that served me well.

I discovered that I am the most reliable source of love, guidance, and support for myself. I realize now that what I originally sought from others actually exists inside me.

Others may, at times, offer information or resources that can be helpful. I will carefully consider how each offer fits for me, by testing its alignment with loving myself and wanting only the best for myself.

I will love and support others when I feel joy in doing so. In this way, I give to sustain myself and not as a sacrifice.

I will continue to use my Five Steps of Emotional Self-Reliance to support myself and make decisions in my best interest. I hope that others will also choose to find their own way, based on these Five Steps, and experience the peace of being at one with their heart's desire.

I have finally grown up and left home.

The Five-Step Practice of Emotional Self-Reliance

This Practice builds on the information, life lessons, and personal practices conveyed in "The Journey" and its accompanying commentary. The Five-Step Practice of Emotional Self-Reliance is not a one-time practice, but rather a lifelong journey to develop an internal source of support and guidance to help you find your own way.

"I will do it myself."

Five Steps of Emotional Self-Reliance

Step 1: "I love you."

*Loving yourself is a heartfelt feeling first
generated and then received by you.*

Step 2: "I want only the best for you."

*Wanting only the best for yourself is an attitude of support and encouragement
similar to what might come from a helpful parent, teacher, friend, or guide.*

Step 3: "I listen carefully to your heart's desire."

*Listening carefully to your heart's desire is a choice
to find direction based on the guidance of your heart.*

Step 4: "I support your heart's desire
with my best resources."

*Supporting your heart's desire with your best energy, power,
and resources is an action to invest wisely in yourself.*

Step 5: "I will stay with you in success and failure."

*Staying with yourself in success and failure is a lifelong commitment to
loving yourself, wanting only the best for yourself, listening carefully to your
heart's desire, and supporting your heart's desire with your best resources.*

Step 1 Practice
Loving Yourself

Loving yourself is a heartfelt feeling first generated and then received by you.

In this practice you will learn to generate a feeling of love in your heart and then apply this love to yourself. This fundamental task of learning to love yourself can be difficult and may at first feel unnatural. If you become confused, frustrated, or discouraged, you may be tempted to give up. Have compassion for yourself if you find yourself struggling. Take a break away from the present task to do something enjoyable and come back later when you are ready.

This practice will be one of our longest because experiencing love for ourselves can be one of the most challenging aspects of our lives. It is not learned in a day but is developed over time with consistent practice. This is a lifelong process, so do not be discouraged if this does not all happen at once.

It is important to set aside some time—at least 15 minutes—and choose a quiet, peaceful space where you will not be interrupted. You will need a comfortable place to lie down. As you go through the following instructions, it is helpful to pause at the end of each direction to integrate in your body what you are being asked to do. Consider making a recording of the following instructions to play back to yourself.

Let's begin!

Phase 1: Relax Your Body

1. *Lie on your back* and place your hands over your upper chest.

2. *Breathe slowly and deeply* in a relaxed manner to increase your body awareness.

3. *Allow your muscles to relax* with long slow exhales.

4. *Silently say to yourself* "I am" with each inhale, and then say "relaxed" with each exhale.

5. *Pay particular attention to the brief pause* between each exhale and the following inhale.

6. *Imagine a small window or door that opens* to you during this pause.

7. *Picture this opening as a passageway* to move deeper into your experience of relaxation and letting go.

Phase 2: Generate Love in Your Heart

1. *Breathe into your upper chest* to increase awareness of your heart.

2. *Imagine your heart expanding and full of love.* Take a few moments to experience the effects of this visualization.

3. *Direct your attention to someone you love* most dearly—a parent, a child, a partner, a pet, or perhaps a spiritual guide.

4. *Bring this loved individual into your awareness* by visualizing their face or an aspect of them that opens your heart with warmth. Feel your love for them openly and allow your heart to expand.

Phase 3: Transfer the Warm Feeling of Love from Your Heart through Your Arms to Your Hands

When you experience this warm, opening sensation of love in your heart . . .

1. *Imagine this warmth passing through your arms* to your hands with each exhale. As you feel this movement of warming energy . . .

2. *Remove your hands from your chest* and place them by your sides with your palms up.

3. *Relax and soften your open hands* with each gentle exhale. The more you can relax and let go, the more loving warmth is transferred from your heart to your hands.

4. *Imagine your hands heating up,* as if you have placed them in warm water.

Phase 4: Imagine Reaching Out with Open Hands to Hold an Infant

1. *Slowly move your arms and hands upward and inward* from your sides until your palms are directly facing each other in front of your chest.

2. *Experiment with moving your palms closer together* and then farther apart until you feel the best warm, energetic connection between the palms of your hands.

3. *Now imagine what it would feel like to reach out* to hold a newborn child in your hands. (If you are unfamiliar with this experience, picture a small puppy or kitten to get this feeling of reaching out to hold something new, soft, fresh, and alive.)

4. *Allow your fingers to warm and expand,* as you imagine making contact with this precious newborn.

5. *Imagine holding and supporting this being* directly in front of you, as if you are the first to welcome them to the planet.

6. *Exhale and enjoy this experience,* as you drop deeper into a feeling of love and respect for this newborn.

Phase 5: Make Contact from Your Heart through Your Hands to Your Chest

1. *Imagine the infant you are holding is you,* perfect in every way and not yet changed by the world. As you feel this loving warmth in your open hands...

2. *Imagine slowly bringing this infant closer* to be held against your heart, as you move your palms in toward your upper chest.

3. *Then allow your open hands to make soft contact* with your upper chest.

4. *Pause and exhale* as you hold this being who is you.

5. *Connect this loving feeling* coming from your heart through your hands to this newly arrived child who just happens to be you.

6. *Softly say, "I love you,"* and then say your name.

7. *Try saying this phrase in different tones and cadences* to feel which is your most effective way to express this message authentically and to enhance the connection.

Phase 6: Receive the Warm Loving Contact

1. *Now switch your attention to be the receiver* of this warm, loving contact.

2. *Open your chest and soak up the warmth* from your hands, like a pleasant bath.

3. *Softly adjust your palms and fingertips* on your upper chest to enhance the feeling of being held securely and loved.

4. *Enjoy this connection* between the love you have generated and the young child who is you.

5. *Say, "I love you,"* and then say your name.

6. *Pause briefly after each exhale* to receive this warm loving contact.

When you experience your face softening, your body warming, and perhaps gentle tears of recognition, you know you are there.

Phase 7: Historical Review and Forgiveness

After you have had some success in generating a feeling of love in your heart toward this innocent being that is you, begin your chronological journey from infancy to the present. Continue to generate love toward yourself as you recall significant experiences at different stages of your life.

Pay special attention to unique circumstances that create a challenge to feeling loved. You may need to return and review these challenging situations in future practices to establish a reliable source of love for yourself.

It may help to display photographs of yourself at various ages as you learn to love and support yourself openly without judgment.

Begin your chronological journey:

1. *Love yourself as you begin to talk and walk at age one.* Love yourself as you have a misstep and fall down. Appreciate that learning to get up and try again after we fall is one of our early experiences of determination. Express, "I love you," and say the name you were called at age one.

2. *Celebrate your second birthday* as you notice your growing independence and strength to say, "I do it myself!" as only a two-year-old can defiantly express. Keep your heart open and loving toward

yourself as language is mastered and you begin to express what you want.

3. *Remember and enjoy those pre-school moments* of play, curiosity, and laughter. Love that part of yourself that likes to have a good time and laugh out loud when things strike you as funny.

4. *Love yourself for your courage to try new things* by leaving home and beginning elementary school. Notice how you are becoming your own person. Love this new growing identity in yourself. Also love yourself in the moments when you remember feeling anxious or afraid. Comfort yourself by saying, "I love you and it will be okay," and say your name.

5. *Reassure yourself and keep your heart open* toward your young self when mistakes are made or embarrassments felt. Know that you are lovable just as you are, even when you have a lot to learn.

6. *Continue on in this manner of loving yourself* as you review significant experiences from childhood, through adolescence, to the present. Include birthdays, graduations, accomplishments, family events, traumas, losses, and other conditions or events that impacted you.

- *Be there to hold and love yourself* without reservation, especially when you were hurt, discouraged, or made to feel wrong. Say, "I love you" and repeat your name. Know that you made your best decisions at the time given your limited information and experience.

- *If you remember an unresolved conflict,* this is a good time to state the event out loud and acknowledge whatever responsibility you had in the event. Then express from your heart, "I love you and forgive you," and say your name.

- *Love yourself through your disappointments,* successes, and failures that have brought you to this present moment.

7. *Really feel what it is like to be seen, held, and loved* so completely. Please exhale and know you are loved.

8. *Celebrate your life by filling your heart with love,* appreciation, and respect for yourself. Only you know how far you have come with the handicaps you experienced.

Continue this practice of loving yourself on a daily basis as you face challenging situations and important decisions.

Step 2 Practice
Wanting Only the Best for Yourself

*Wanting only the best for yourself is an attitude of support
and encouragement similar to what might come from
a helpful parent, teacher, friend, or guide.*

Step 2 is best practiced in conjunction with Step 1.

1. *Step 1:* With your hands over your heart, generate
   a feeling of love for yourself and then receive this
   heartfelt love, as outlined in Step 1 Practice.

   - *Repeat several times, "I love you"* and then say
     your name.

   - *Allow the warmth* of this heartfelt statement to
     fill your chest.

2. *Step 2:* In the same way you would naturally want
   only the best for someone you love, direct this
   attitude of support and encouragement toward
   yourself.

   - *Repeat several times, "I love you and want only the
     best for you"* and then say your name.

   - *Exhale, relax, and take your time* to feel this
     emotional support and encouragement.

In addition to emotional support, Steps 1 and 2 provide guidance for decision making. When you are considering a decision, it is helpful to check if your choice is consistent with the feeling of really loving yourself, as well as the attitude of wanting only the best for yourself. It is important that you do not cheat yourself; your conclusion must truly be in your best interest in the long run, not just a momentary high without regard for the long-term consequences. Loving and encouraging yourself, making decisions, and then taking responsibility by living with the consequences are all part of Emotional Self-Reliance.

3. *Application for decision making:* With the feeling and attitude generated and received in Steps 1 and 2, say the following, "I love you [say your name] and I want only the best for you. Therefore, I recommend . . ."

   - *Pause* to allow a possible conclusion, direction, or decision about a current situation to come into your awareness.

   - *State* this conclusion out loud.

4. *Testing new conclusions:* By *listening* to the conclusion generated from Steps 1 and 2, you become the *receiver* of your own "advice." It is important to then pay attention to the responses of your body to determine if this advice rings true for you. You will know when a conclusion or piece of advice fits for you when:

- There is warmth welling up in your chest.
- You are flooded with a sense of support and feeling of hope.
- You have tears of recognition that express, "This is it!"
- You feel relief as you exhale.
- You are energized to take action.

Note: It can be helpful to try several different conclusions to sense which recommendation is most aligned with your sense of love and wanting only the best for yourself. Remember you are constantly evolving, so this is not a one-time trial. Sometimes multiple tries over several days will give you a more consistent reading of what is truly in your best interest. Other times you may miss the mark and need to make mid-course corrections to better align yourself with your love and wanting only the best for yourself. Have compassion for yourself when errors are made and try again.

When we recognize the truth for ourselves and feel determined to stand by it, the energy of our body is ignited. When we further acknowledge this truth in words, "Yes, this is it!" we feel empowered and encouraged to move forward.

Step 3 Practice
Listening Carefully to Your Heart's Desire

*Listening carefully to your heart's desire is a choice
to find direction based on the guidance of your heart.*

Set aside about 15 minutes and find a comfortable place
to sit or lie down. Begin with the following warm-up
practices you have already learned:

1. *Listen to the sounds around you* to become more present.

2. *Relax yourself* from head to toe.

3. *Bring up the feeling of love for yourself* and the
   attitude of wanting only the best for yourself.

4. *Repeat several times, "I love you and want only the best
   for you"* and then say your name.

When you are present and relaxed with a feeling of
love and support for yourself, continue by listening
carefully to your heart's desire:

1. *Focus your attention in your upper chest* by resting your
   hands directly over your heart and exhaling softly.

2. *Hold yourself gently to nurture and heal* as you listen
   carefully for your heart's desire.

3. *Have the conscious intent of going deeper inside* with each exhale to contact and understand your deepest longing.

4. *Ask yourself, "What do I really want?"* The first response is often a good indication.

5. *You can go deeper with repeated questions* of, "Okay, but what do I really want, if there were no restrictions of time, money, or practicality?"

6. *If you do not at first recognize your heart's desire:*

   • *Remain curious* to discover it.

   • *Keep your heart open* throughout the day to notice any activity, image, story, or idea that speaks to you and inspires your interest or excitement.

7. *When you discover a possible heart's desire,* vocalize it in a relaxed state without distractions to feel if it rings true for you.

8. *When you say the truth of your heart's desire,* your body softens and tension is released. It is as if your body says, "Yes, that's it! That is what I really want."

9. *Notice if you feel more peaceful,* energized, and a growing sense of joy when saying what you desire. These are signs you are coming closer to representing your deepest heart's desire.

10. *To find direction in your life*, state this choice to yourself, "I listen carefully to your heart's desire," and say your name.

Step 4 Practice

Supporting Your Heart's Desire with Your Best Resources

Supporting your heart's desire with your best energy, power, and resources is an action to invest wisely in yourself.

Once you have identified your heart's desire through your Step 3 Practice:

1. *Consider how you can be the best benefactor* providing for your heart's desire. After careful appraisal and consideration of what you need to support your heart's desire...

2. *Determine what resources you have available.* These may include energy, time, education, or money.

3. *Make a wise investment decision* in support of your heart's desire, keeping in mind the resources you may need to reserve for other aspects of your life.

4. *Take one step today* toward investing in your heart's desire.

5. *Affirm to yourself,* "I support your heart's desire with my best resources," and say your name.

Step 5 Practice
Staying with Yourself in Success and Failure

*Staying with yourself in success and failure is a lifelong
commitment to loving yourself, wanting only the best
for yourself, listening carefully to your heart's desire, and
supporting your heart's desire with your best resources.*

1. *Learn to support yourself during your darkest hour,* as
   you look directly at defeat or loss by implementing
   your steps of Emotional Self-Reliance.

2. *Be there for yourself when others are not available,*
   refuse to help, or turn against you.

3. *Keep this personal commitment* of support for yourself
   during changing conditions.

4. *State this lifelong commitment to yourself,* "I will stay
   with you in success and failure," and say your name.

5. *Take action on a daily basis* in support of this
   commitment.

THE FIVE-STEP PRACTICE OF • EMOTIONAL SELF-RELIANCE ™

I stay with you in success & failure

I want only the best for you

I Love You

I support you with my best resources

I listen to your heart's desire

EMOTIONALSELFRELIANCE.COM

Acknowledgments

I deeply appreciate the patients in my psychotherapy practice and the workshop participants in Brazil who were willing to learn the Five-Step Practice of Emotional Self-Reliance during the past 15 years. Through their subsequent growth and healing, I was shown the usefulness and power of this Five-Step process for many individuals facing various challenges. The positive feedback from these individuals encouraged me to further develop the Five-Step Practice and ultimately to write this book.

This is a book about self-reliance. When we are learning to rely on ourselves, there are often helpers along the way. They advise us, help us see ourselves more clearly, and provide guidance.

The following acquaintances, friends, relatives, patients, and colleagues showed up during the process of writing this book: Ami, Barbara, Bob, Catherine, Chris, Diane, Edmundo, Elaine, Juliette, Leda, Martina, Robin, Sally, Stan, and Vanessa. They read various versions of the manuscript, provided feedback, and/or offered encouragement. Some were also willing subjects to try out the Five-Step Practice. I thank them for their help and sincerely appreciate their honest and thoughtful input.

I would like to specifically thank two trusted friends and respected colleagues: Douglas K. Smith, PhD. and Allan Gerson, PhD. They reviewed the manuscript and offered insightful comments and suggestions.

A heartfelt thank you to Casey DeFranco, who provided professional editing, guidance, and encouragement on this project.

I also would like to express my thanks to the artists who gave permission to use their artwork. Their names are listed with their artwork in Artists' Credits.

The most important thank you goes to Amy Hermann. She arrived in my life as a free gift. She is a trusted companion and the love of my life. She has worked side by side with me on this project for the past ten years, exchanging ideas, providing detailed editing of the story, and assisting me in developing the commentary. She also offered creative input and guidance about organization, imagery, and overall presentation of the material. I cannot say enough about her willingness to work hard on the details and manage the production of this project.

And finally, thank *you* for picking up this book and being willing to try something new.

Artists' Credits

1. At Home in the Village
Artist: Gerry Schroeder
Title: First Footprints
Zen Circle: Olga_C/Shutterstock.com

2. Shame
Photographer: Amy Hermann
Title: Ali's Dog Feeling Shame

3. Lost and Confused
Photographer: Amy Hermann
Title: Rug Pattern, Artist Unknown

4. Listening as a Key to Being Present
Photographer: Amy Hermann
Title: Gaia Stream

5. Expressing Anger
Artist: Chris Pavlov (a.k.a. Krste Pavlov)
Title: Magic Carpet Ride
(Image is a small section of painting)

6. Learning from Experience
Photographer: Amy Hermann
Title: River Rocks

7. A Test of Confidence
Artist: Michelle Dujardin/zendrawing.com
Title: Sequoia

8. Swallowed Identity
Photographer: Devin Koob/
Shutterstock.com

9. Identity Based on Experience
Artist: Robin Fayer
Title: Target

10. Trapped by Fear and Group Identity
Artist: Ann Raleigh
Title: School of Fish

11. The Little Red Hen
Artist: Helen K. Davie
Title: The Little Red Hen

12. I Will Do It Myself
Artist: Helen K. Davie
Title: I Will Do It Myself
(Also similar line drawing, p. 202)

13. Fear of the Unknown
Photographer: Gerry Schroeder
Title: Footprints

14. It Is Never Completely Safe
Photographer: Amy Hermann
Title: Rattlesnake

15. Relaxation
Photographer: Gerry Schroeder
Title: Guan Yin, Artist Unknown

16. Alert and Focused with Purpose
Photographer: BG Smith/
Shutterstock.com

17. Things Do Not Always Go as Planned
Photographer: Amy Hermann
Title: Man in the Maze, Artist Unknown

18. Recovery
Photographer: Amy Hermann
Title: Lotus

19. Sadness and Loss
Photographer: Amy Hermann
Title: Hollow Tree

20. Loving Yourself
Photographer: Gerry Schroeder
Title: Manzanita Heart

21. Imagining the Future
Artist: Robin Fayer
Title: Imagining the Future

22. Wanting the Best for Yourself
Photographer: Amy Hermann
Title: Bursting Open

23. From Fear to Curiosity
Photographer: Amy Hermann
Title: Following the Stream

24. Discovering the Treasure
Photographer: Amy Hermann
Title: Discovering the Treasure

25. The Poisonous Attack
Photographer: Amy Hermann
Title: Tree Silhouette

26. Standing Up for Yourself
Artist: Nannette Domingos
Title: Horses

27. Being Called Selfish
Photographer: Gerry Schroeder
Title: Beeing Selfish

28. Listening to Your Heart's Desire
Photographer: Ansley Braverman
ansleybraverman.com
Title: Hands on Heart (Persian, 2500–2300 BC)

29. The Surprise Opportunity
Photographer: Amy Hermann
Title: Leaf Package

30. Supporting Your Heart's Desire
Artist: Amy Hermann
Title: Basket with Acorns

31. The Free Gift
Artist: Tiel Larson
Title: Leather Pouch

32. The Commitment to Yourself
Photographer: Amy Hermann
Title: Gold Ring

33. Anticipation
Photographer: MagicBones/
Shutterstock.com

34. Taking the Plunge
Photographer: Amy Hermann
Title: Taking the Plunge

Reflections
Photographer: Gerry Schroeder
Title: Reflections

Dedication
Photographer: Shana Schank
Caption: One-year-old Elijah reaching for his heart's desire, as Ruby reaches back to make contact.

Dedication

To my horse, Ruby

You were the burning dream of the five-year-old boy in me.
You arrived in my life over 60 years later—against all odds.
In the short four-and-a-half years we had together before
your untimely death, you fulfilled my deepest heart's desire.

About the Author

Gerry Schroeder, PhD (a.k.a. Gerald Lynn Schroeder) is a clinical psychologist who has been in private practice in Santa Barbara, California, since 1976. Originally from Hillsboro, Kansas, he received his doctorate in clinical psychology from the University of Kansas in 1973.

Dr. Schroeder specializes in body-centered psychotherapy— focusing on breath, movement, muscle tension, posture, and body awareness to gain insight into psychological trauma and to guide patients toward greater health and well-being. He is a passionate catalyst for personal growth, healing, and transformation.

Outside his clinical work, Gerry is an avid horseman— having recently fulfilled his lifelong heart's desire of working with horses. He lives near Santa Barbara, California.

Made in the USA
Coppell, TX
27 February 2020